Unfolding the Living Word

Unfolding the Living Word

*New Kyries, Canticles, Gospel Acclamations
and Collects for Holy Communion
Years A, B & C*

Jim Cotter

CANTERBURY PRESS
Norwich

In association with
Cairns Publications
Aberdaron

© Jim Cotter 2012

First published in 2012 by Canterbury Press

Editorial office
Invicta House, 108–114 Golden Lane
London, EC1Y 0TG

Canterbury Press is an imprint of Hymns Ancient and Modern Ltd
(a registered charity)
13a Hellesdon Park Road, Norwich, Norfolk, NR6 5DR

www.canterburypress.co.uk

All rights reserved. No part of this publication may be reproduced, stored in a retrieval system, or transmitted, in any form or by any means, electronic, mechanical, photocopying or otherwise, without the prior permission of the publisher, SCM Press.

Jim Cotter has asserted his right under the Copyright, Designs and Patents Act, 1988, to be identified as the Author of this Work

British Library Cataloguing in Publication data

A catalogue record for this book is available
from the British Library

978 1 84825 275 2

Typeset by Regent Typesetting, London
Printed and bound by
CPI Group (UK) Ltd, Croydon

Contents

Introduction	xi
Sources, Echoes and Acknowledgements	xv
The First Sunday of Advent	2
The Second Sunday of Advent	7
The Third Sunday of Advent	13
The Fourth Sunday of Advent	18
Christmas Eve	23
Christmas Night	26
Christmas Morning	29
Christmas Day	32
The First Sunday of Christmas	35
The Second Sunday of Christmas	39
Collects for Weekdays during the Christmas Season	42
The Epiphany	46
The First Sunday of Epiphany	48
The Second Sunday of Epiphany	53
The Third Sunday of Epiphany	58
The Fourth Sunday of Epiphany	62
The Feast of the Presentation of Christ in the Temple	66
The Fifth Sunday before Lent	68
The Fourth Sunday before Lent	72
The Third Sunday before Lent	77
The Second Sunday before Lent	81
The Sunday next before Lent	87
Ash Wednesday	91

The First Sunday of Lent	102
The Second Sunday of Lent	107
The Third Sunday of Lent	112
The Fourth Sunday of Lent – Mothering Sunday	117
The Fifth Sunday of Lent	122
Palm Sunday	127
Monday of Holy Week	131
Tuesday of Holy Week	134
Wednesday of Holy Week	137
Maundy Thursday	140
Good Friday	143
Easter Eve	149
Easter Day	151
The Second Sunday of Easter	155
The Third Sunday of Easter	159
The Fourth Sunday of Easter	164
The Fifth Sunday of Easter	169
The Sixth Sunday of Easter	173
Ascension Day	176
The Seventh Sunday of Easter	179
Pentecost	183
Trinity Sunday	189
The Sunday between 29 May and 4 June	194
The Sunday between 5 and 11 June	198
The Sunday between 12 and 18 June	202
The Sunday between 19 and 25 June	207
The Sunday between 26 June and 2 July	211
The Sunday between 3 and 9 July	216
The Sunday between 10 and 16 July	220
The Sunday between 17 and 23 July	224
The Sunday between 24 and 30 July	228
The Sunday between 31 July and 6 August	232
The Sunday between 7 and 13 August	237
The Sunday between 14 and 20 August	241

The Sunday between 21 and 27 August	245
The Sunday between 28 August and 3 September	249
The Sunday between 4 and 10 September	254
The Sunday between 11 and 17 September	258
The Sunday between 18 and 24 September	263
The Sunday between 25 September and 1 October	268
The Sunday between 2 and 8 October	272
The Sunday between 9 and 15 October	277
The Sunday between 16 and 22 October	282
The Sunday between 23 and 29 October	286
The Fourth Sunday before Advent	291
Collects for weekdays between 30 October and 14 November	296
All Saints' Day	303
All Souls' Day	306
The Third Sunday before Advent	309
The Second Sunday before Advent	314
The Sunday next before Advent	319

Appendices

1 A sample order of service for Holy Communion	325
2 A sample order of service for Morning Prayer	336
3 Praying for Others: Intercession	345
4 An Ecumenical order of service for the Blessed Communion	349
5 Some miscellaneous collects	376

Dedication

*For Hywyn's people,
the congregation of the church at Aberdaron
and those who visit as guests and pilgrims*

*With gratitude
for their patient willingness
to be challenged
and, I hope, encouraged and consoled,
in the years in which most of what is gathered in this book
was tried and tested.*

Introduction

There is considerable agreement among most churches about the structure of the service that is still variously called the Lord's Supper, the Holy Communion, the Eucharist, the Mass. For the Church of England, *Common Worship* lays it out succinctly on page 166:

> The people and the priest
>> greet each other in the Lord's name
>> confess their sins and are assured of God's forgiveness
>> keep silence and pray a Collect
>> proclaim and respond to the word of God
>> pray for the Church and the world
>> exchange the Peace
>> prepare the table
>> pray the Eucharistic Prayer
>> break the bread
>> receive communion
>> depart with God's blessing

Within each section there may well be alternatives. Indeed the book provides eight eucharistic prayers. (No wonder, compared with the *Book of Common Prayer*, the books we have to carry around with us make us stagger and yearn for a sturdy shopping trolley.) Even so, each alternative must have a thread or threads in common with the others. There is a core which *shall* be said or done, in order that the service can be recognized as authentic by other congregations and churches.

INTRODUCTION

However, there are other variants which *may* be used. Within *Common Worship* these include: hymn, welcome (p.167); prayer of preparation, Commandments, Beatitudes, Comfortable Words, Summary of the Law (p.168); Kyrie eleison (p.170); Gloria (p.171); response to readings, hymns and songs between readings, Gospel Acclamation (p.172); introduction to the Peace, an exchange of peace, hymn, gathering of gifts, prayer at the preparation of the table (p.175); Agnus Dei (p.179); hymns and anthems during distribution (p.181); hymn (p.183).

This book is a contribution to the material that may be used. It is offered in the spirit of hymn writers, and of hymn editors who often make changes to the original, leaving out verses, altering words and phrases. Each Sunday of the year has its own suggestions, for the Kyrie eleison, for a Canticle (sometimes a response or a hymn or a reflection), for the Gospel Acclamation, and for a Collect which could be used at the end of the sermon or after the distribution of communion.

The Kyries

By custom the response is usually threefold: Kyrie eleison, Christe eleison, Kyrie eleison. In this book, there is a line of confession before each response, neither too generalized as to have no bite nor too specific to be justifiably ignored by some or most of those present. (New contributions to liturgy have to be neither too conformist nor too individualistic, with less freedom than the poets but more than the fundamentalists – who are alive and well in liturgical discourse as well as in biblical discourse.) The words could be said by one voice or by the whole congregation.

There are numerous musical settings for the responses. One is included in this book, in Appendix 4, which sets the Jesus Prayer in Greek to a simple chant (p. 353). It is home-made.

INTRODUCTION

The Canticles, Responses, Hymns, and Reflections

Most of the canticles offered in this book have not been published before. A few come from *Out of the Silence ... Into the Silence*, a book for daily prayer. They are neither translations nor paraphrases, but 'unfoldings'. Occasionally there is a response or a reflection or a hymn. They are intended for use between readings.

The Gospel Acclamations

The wording does not strictly follow that laid down in *Common Worship*, but I hope it is in accord with it. (Yes, I know I am tweaking a *shall* section.) Again, a simple chant for the lines of Alleluias is suggested in Appendix 4 (p. 357) – it is also homemade.

Each acclamation is given its own line, resonating in some way with the particular reading that follows. At the end, after the final Alleluias, the reader or cantor turns to the preacher to say or sing the last line: 'Unfold the Living Word for us today.'

Collects

The norm in what is provided here is six collects for each week, one for each of Years A, B, and C, plus three others, perhaps therefore one for each day of the week, the seventh repeating the one for the current year. In use, the tone of voice for these prayers is quiet and reflective, making them more meditation than declamation.

Some of the collects, sometimes revised or adapted, first appeared as prayers at the end of the psalms in *Out of the Silence ... Into the Silence*.

INTRODUCTION

The Appendices

These are counterpoint to the rest of the book. The first two illustrate one way of incorporating material from it into Sunday services of either Holy Communion or Morning Prayer. The third gives some suggestions for the prayer for others, which in practice often needs more restraint than usual in the number of words used. After all, it comes almost immediately after the monologue of the sermon, and it seems to me it works better if the leader of the prayer invites us to pray by giving us some prompts and leaving us awhile in silence.

The fourth appendix does not find a comfortable home within the provisions of *Common Worship*, and indeed that is not its function. It is 'work in process', an order for Holy Communion, entitled The Blessed Communion, which is a literal translation into English from the official title used by the Church in Wales, Y Cymun Bendigaid. (Incorporated in the text is a chant for 'Dona nobis pacem'. It is years since I came across it and I'm not at all sure who composed it. My memory tells me that I was told that it was by Mozart. If any reader definitely knows the source, I'd be glad to be informed.) The service has been celebrated on retreats, for parish weekends, at conferences, and in homes. It is ecumenical in intent. Hundreds of people have participated over the years, and scores have made helpful suggestions. The material in this book, therefore, easily falls into place in this experimental though ecumenical liturgy. Its subtitle aims to be catholic in the most generous meaning of that word, Here Comes Everybody.

Jim Cotter

Aberdaron, July 2012

Sources, Echoes and Acknowledgements

First Sunday of Advent
  Canticle: Isaiah 11
  Collect 4: *Book of Common Prayer*, adapted
Second Sunday of Advent
  Canticle: Isaiah 40
Christmas Eve
  Canticle: Isaiah 9
First Sunday of Christmas
  Canticle: John 1.1–14, unfolded
The Epiphany
  Canticle: Isaiah 60
The Second Sunday of Epiphany
  Canticle: Isaiah 60; Revelation 22
The Presentation, 2 February
  Canticle: Nunc Dimittis, unfolded
The Fourth Sunday before Lent
  Reflection: Based on J.D. Crossan, *The Historical Jesus*, p. 270, T & T Clark, 1953, *The Essential Jesus*, Harper Collins 1995, pp. 58, 63, 90, 123
The Sunday next before Lent
  Canticle: The Transfiguration 2 Corinthians 4
  Collect Year A: 2 Peter 1.19
Monday of Holy Week to Good Friday
  Reflection: Based on the 'seven last words' of Jesus on the cross, as given to us by the four writers of the Gospels
The Fourth Sunday of Easter
  Canticle: Unfolded from the Easter Anthems in the *Book of Common Prayer*
Ascension Day
  Canticle: Unfolded from 1 Timothy 3.16

SOURCES, ECHOES AND ACKNOWLEDGEMENTS

Pentecost
  Collect for the week following Pentecost: unfolded from the Confirmation Prayer in the *Book of Common Prayer*
Sundays between 12 and 18 June
  Collect Year A: The dynamic of the 'Kingdom of God', according to J. D. Crossan, *The Historical Jesus*, p. 332
The Sunday between 26 June and 2 July
  Kyries: Slightly adapted from J. D. Crossan & Jonathan Reed, *In Search of Paul*, HarperSanFrancisco, 2004, p. 377
The Sundays between 7 and 13 August, 14 and 20 August, 21 and 27 August
  Reflection: Based on insights of William McNamara of the Spiritual Life Institute, Crestone, Colorado, USA
The Sunday between 28 August and 3 September
  Reflection: 1 Corinthians 13
The Sunday between 4 and 10 September
  Reflection: Luke 6. 27–28, 36–38
The Sunday between 11 and 17 September
  Kyries: The first two lines are from Sogyal Rinpoche, *The Tibetan Book of Living and Dying*
The Sunday between 25 September and 1 October
  Reflection: Ephesians 3.16–19
  Collect 6: Lines 10–13 echo words of Dag Hammerskjold in *Markings*, Faber, 1964, p. 87
The Sunday between 9 and 15 October
  Reflection: An expanded meditation on The Lord's Prayer
The Sunday between 23 and 29 October
  Collect Year C: Line 7–9: Micah 6–8
The Fourth Sunday before Advent, All Saints' Day
  Canticle: Revelation 2–3, variously
All Souls' Day
  Canticle: Revelation 21.1–5
  Collect: Based on a prayer by John V. Taylor in *The Primal Vision*, SCM Press, 1963, p. 169
The Third Sunday before Advent
  Canticle: Romans 8.38–39
Christ the King: The Sunday next before Advent
  Responses: Based on The Lord's Prayer as unfolded by J. D. Crossan in *The Greatest Prayer*
Appendix 1
  The Preparation of the Table: 3rd section by compiler;
  The Giving of Communion: lines 6 & 7: St Augustine of Hippo

New Kyries, Canticles, Gospel Acclamations and Collects for Holy Communion Years A, B & C

The First Sunday of Advent

Kyries

We have been afraid of the fierceness of your love,
which sears our hearts as with a laser.

We have refused to believe that you are gentle in judgement,
that your hands loosen the knots of our bitterness.

We have failed to see that your eyes are wise in discernment,
that your justice restores us and heals.

Response/Canticle/Hymn/Reflection

From the stump of an old gnarled tree,
a new shoot will yet spring forth.
From roots hidden deep in the ground,
a sapling will grow again.

The Spirit of God will rest upon you,
the spirit of wisdom and understanding,
the spirit of counsel and might,
the spirit of knowledge and godly fear.

You will not judge by what your ears hear,
nor decide by what your eyes see.
You will judge the poor with justice,
and defend the humble of the land with equity.

THE FIRST SUNDAY OF ADVENT

Your mouth will be a rod to strike down the ruthless,
and with a word you will devastate the wicked.
Round your waist you will wear the belt of justice,
and good faith will be the girdle round your body.

Then the wolf will dwell with the sheep,
and the leopard will lie down with the kid;
the calf and the young lion will grow up together,
and a little child will lead them.

The cow and the bear will feed
and their young will lie down together.
The lion will eat straw like cattle;
the infant will play over the hole of the cobra,
and the young child dance over the viper's nest.

They will not hurt or destroy in all your holy mountain,
for the earth will be full of the knowledge of God
as the waters cover the sea.

Gospel Acclamation

Alleluia, alleluia, alleluia.
Alleluia, alleluia, alleluia.

Keep awake. Be alert.
Open your eyes – look – and see!
Open your ears – listen – and hear!
Keep awake. Be alert.
You do not know when the time will come.
Alleluia, alleluia, alleluia.

A reading from the Gospel according to Matthew/Mark/Luke
Alleluia, alleluia, alleluia.

THE FIRST SUNDAY OF ADVENT

A   *Matthew 24.36–44*
B   *Mark 13.24–37*
C   *Luke 21.25–36*

Give glory to the living God.
Alleluia, alleluia, alleluia.
Unfold the Living Word for us today.

Collects

Year A

Living Presence of truth,
   whose word resounds
      amid the clamour of our violence,
keep your households watchful,
   aware of the hour in which we live,
and hasten the day when the sounds of war
   will be for ever stilled,
the powers of evil scattered,
and the earth and its peoples gathered into one.
We pray this through the One
   in whose constant coming we trust,
   whose day is always near.

Year B

Living Presence, utterly truthful,
   of whom we are aware at times we least expect,
   revealed in people we have judged least likely,
keep us watchful and expectant,
   ready to be needled into repentance
   and surprised into joy.
We pray this through the One
   in whose constant coming we trust,
   whose day is always near.

THE FIRST SUNDAY OF ADVENT

Year C

Living Presence of fierce love and gentle judgement,
   our doom and our deliverance,
     searing us and healing us
        who have become forgetful of your ways
        and dulled by our selfish desires,
keep us alert and attentive to your word,
make us holy and faithful to your way,
    that we may stand firm
       when the winds howl and the foundations shake.
We pray this through the One
   in whose constant coming we trust,
   whose day is always near.

4

Living Presence, all-powerful in love,
give us grace to cast away the works of evil
   and put upon us the armour of the good,
now in the time of this earthly life,
   in which in Jesus Christ
      you came to us in great humility,
that on the last day,
   when you will reveal yourself to us in greatest glory,
we may rise to the fullness of life eternal,
through the same Jesus Christ,
   in whom our humanity is transformed for ever.

THE FIRST SUNDAY OF ADVENT

5

Living Presence,
　powerfully in love with us
　and with the universe of your creating,
give us such a sense of your presence
　that we may be stripped of greed and fear,
　　and be clothed with generosity and compassion
　　　towards all the peoples and creatures of the earth,
now, in the time left to us,
　that at the last,
　　when you will reveal yourself to us
　　　as terrible and utter beauty,
　　we shall know ourselves and all the universe
　　　transformed to glory.
We pray this through the One
　whose humanity is transfigured,
　whose being is vibrant with your Spirit,
　and who dwells for ever in your heart.

6

Living Presence, fierce, fiery, loving,
come with burning coals to purge our lips;
come with the judgement that saves,
　and give us back our sense of worth
　because it matters what we do;
come with passionate desire
　and sweep us into your arms;
come with the love that will not let us go.
We pray this through the One
　in whose constant coming we trust,
　whose day is always near.

The Second Sunday of Advent

Kyries

We have been afraid of the fierceness of your love,
which sears our hearts as with a laser.

We have refused to believe that you are gentle in judgement,
that your hands loosen the knots of our bitterness.

We have failed to see that your eyes are wise in discernment,
that your justice restores us and heals.

Response/Canticle/Hymn/Reflection

Give comfort to my people, says your God.
Speak tenderly to the city, to Jerusalem.
Announce this news to them all:

**Your rebellion is ended,
your iniquity is pardoned,
your slavery is abolished,
your imprisonment is over.**

A voice cries:
In the wilderness prepare the way of the Living One:
make straight in the desert a highway for our God.
Every valley will be lifted up,
and every mountain and hill be made low;

THE SECOND SUNDAY OF ADVENT

the uneven ground will become level,
and the rough places a plain.
And the glory of the Living God will be revealed.

So have I heard,
and so do I announce to all who will listen.

A voice said to me,
Cry!

And I said,
What shall I cry?

All flesh is grass,
and its beauty is like the flower of the field.
The grass withers and the flower fades,
when the wind of our God blows upon it.
Surely you are like grass.
The grass withers, the flower fades,
but the word of our God will stand for ever.

A voice said to me,
Get you up to a high mountain,
herald of good tidings to Zion;
lift up your voice with strength,
herald of good news to Jerusalem:
Lift it up, fear not:
say to the cities of Judah,
Behold your God!

Gospel Acclamation

Alleluia, alleluia, alleluia.
Alleluia, alleluia, alleluia.

THE SECOND SUNDAY OF ADVENT

Listen to the prophets,
who see what you do not see,
who hear what you do not hear,
who point away from themselves,
who bring you close to the Living Word.
Alleluia, alleluia, alleluia.

A reading from the Gospel according to Matthew/Mark/Luke
Alleluia, alleluia, alleluia.

A   *Matthew 3.1–12*
B   *Mark 1.1–8*
C   *Luke 3.1–6*

Give glory to the living God.
Alleluia, alleluia, alleluia.
Unfold the Living Word for us today.

Collects

Year A

Living Presence, wise and discerning,
  whose voice cuts clear through the desert air,
  heralding a new vision of your commonwealth,
give us clarity of sight
  that we may know what we ought to do,
and strength of will
  that we may accomplish it,
so that complacency may yield to courage,
  conflict give way to reconciliation,
and the faces of condemnation
  grow wise with the discerning judgement
  that never forgets mercy.
We pray this through the One
  in whose constant coming we trust,
  whose day is always near.

THE SECOND SUNDAY OF ADVENT

Year B

Living Presence, strong and merciful,
   coming in our midst with transforming power,
make ready a way in our wilderness,
   clear a path in the tangle of our hearts,
that we may become a repentant people
   who hunger and thirst and strive
     for what is just and good.
We pray this through the One
   in whose constant coming we trust,
   whose day is always near.

Year C

Living Presence, panoramic in vision,
   giving us a sense of direction when we are lost,
   gently yet fiercely reorientating us
     from our waywardness,
guide us in the true path,
   and keep us watchful for our neighbours,
   and alert us to our need of them,
that we may begin to discern the beauty
   that comes from your weaving our ragged lives
     into the pattern of a greater whole.
We pray this through the One
   in whose constant coming we trust,
   whose day is always near.

THE SECOND SUNDAY OF ADVENT

4

Living Presence, awesome and truthful,
   casting out from us the ways of wickedness,
   judging us with the piercing eye
      of fierce and tender love,
   clothing us with the garments
      of justice and compassion,
raise us from the depths of deceit, despair, and doom,
that we may greet your every coming with joy,
   on this day,
   through all our days,
   and at the Great Day
      of the Presence of the Living Christ,
      in whose Spirit we pray.

5

Living Presence of liberating truth,
   sending to us your messengers the prophets
   to turn us around
      and prepare us to receive our liberation,
give us the humility, the insight, and the grace
   to listen to their warnings,
   and to heed the still small voice
      that whispers in our hearts,
that we may look once more upon your face
   and greet your every coming with joy.
We pray this in the Spirit of the One
   who lived the truth and set us free.

THE SECOND SUNDAY OF ADVENT

6

Living Presence, seeming absence,
   whose silence makes us wonder
      if you are deaf to our cries,
even if it is the silence
   of listening and suffering,
test our faith and patience
   no more than we can bear,
and be revealed to us
   as the wisdom and discernment
      that comes from the heart of your silence,
   as the judge of the earth
      who cannot fail to do what is right,
      and to make all things well.
We pray this after the pattern of Jesus
   and in the power of the Spirit.

The Third Sunday of Advent

Kyries

We have been afraid of the fierceness of your love,
which sears our hearts as with a laser.

We have refused to believe that you are gentle in judgement,
that your hands loosen the knots of our bitterness.

We have failed to see that your eyes are wise in discernment,
that your justice restores us and heals.

Response/Canticle/Hymn/Reflection

Of John the Baptist

The ancient vision burned through your eyes,
you yearned for freedom from captivity.
Your people of old were burdened by Pharaoh,
held down by Egypt's power.
The people of your time were oppressed by an emperor,
weighed down by the yoke of Rome.
Your voice rang clear in the desert air,
calling them to cross the Jordan again.
They flocked to you in the wilderness,
and assembled on the banks of the river.
You drenched them with water as they passed over,
cleansing their hearts, giving them hope.

THE THIRD SUNDAY OF ADVENT

They returned to their homes, to wait and to pray,
that their deliverer would suddenly come from on high,
the liberator who would crush their enemies,
freeing them from the powers that ensnared them.
They looked for a warrior,
but he did not come.
They longed for a king,
but they were given an outcast.
They expected violence and victory,
they were challenged to pay the cost of justice and peace.
They expected a throne and a parade,
they received a cradle and a cross.

Gospel Acclamation

Alleluia, alleluia, alleluia.
Alleluia, alleluia, alleluia.

Go to the desert places;
enter the wilderness of your hearts.
Hear again the cry of the living God:
Listen! Make ready! Prepare!
Alleluia, alleluia, alleluia.

A reading from the Gospel according to Matthew/John/Luke
Alleluia, alleluia, alleluia.

A   Matthew 3.1–12
B   John 1.6–8,19–28
C   Luke 3.7–18

Give glory to the living God.
Alleluia, alleluia, alleluia.
Unfold the Living Word for us today.

THE THIRD SUNDAY OF ADVENT

Collects

Year A

Living Presence, glorious and wonderful,
   in whose providence
      the desert blooms,
      broken lives are mended,
      and fearful hearts grow strong in faith,
water our cracked and withered land,
   open our eyes to healing tears,
   and soothe our agitated hearts.
We pray this through the One
   in whose constant coming we trust,
   whose day is always near.

Year B

Mysterious Presence,
   very far and very near,
   clearing the wax from our ears,
   removing the cataracts from our eyes,
gently turn us around that we may listen,
   focus our attention that we may see,
   and sponge the hardness from our hearts.
We pray this through the One
   in whose constant coming we trust,
   whose day is always near.

THE THIRD SUNDAY OF ADVENT

Year C

Living Presence, refining fire,
   sweeping away all that is dried and withered,
   purging us of everything that corrupts,
   kindling into life all that has grown cold,
embrace us with such fierce and tender love
   that will never let us go.
We pray this through the One
   in whose constant coming we trust,
   whose day is always near.

4

Living Presence,
   shaking the foundations of the world,
   yet poised with potential for what is new,
   yearning to be born on earth,
be conceived within us now,
   that we may let you grow in our bellies,
      with trembling and anticipation,
   prepared to embrace without terror
      the labour pains of the age to come.
We pray this through the One
   in whose constant coming we trust,
   whose day is always near.

THE THIRD SUNDAY OF ADVENT

5

Living Presence,
   as we wait in these dark days
      silent, yearning, expectant,
      hope flickering yet still alight,
place in our hands
   the lamps of truth and love and courage,
that we may stand firm,
   and strive with those powers
      that rise in the darkness
      with their new and strange demands.
So may the desires of all our hearts
   be fulfilled in the Presence of Jesus,
      the One who was and who is and who shall be
         the Light of the World.

6

Living Presence, awesome and strange,
   entrusting to us the fate
      of the planet that is our home,
   remaining silent when we cry to you for help,
      hidden when we so desperately need your light,
rescue us from the brink of our doom,
   and through us heal the wounded face of the earth.
We pray this in the Spirit of the One
   whose constant coming moves us forward
      in hope and restoration
      and always new beginnings.

The Fourth Sunday of Advent

Kyries

We have been afraid of the fierceness of your love,
which sears our hearts as with a laser.

We have refused to believe that you are gentle in judgement,
that your hands loosen the knots of our bitterness.

We have failed to see that your eyes are wise in discernment,
that your justice restores us and heals.

Response/Canticle/Hymn/Reflection

An unfolding of the Magnificat

My soul-body swells with love of my Creator,
joy fires my heart for my lover, my God.
My beloved has noticed me and loved me,
a nobody from among the powerless poor.

From this time to the end of days,
all generations will call me blessed.
For Love has drawn me from the shadows:
wonderful indeed is the name of our God.

Your lovingkindness embraces those
who are awestruck with wonder and love,

THE FOURTH SUNDAY OF ADVENT

held in eternity's moment in time.
Your gentleness has shown great strength:
the proud have been scattered
in the fantasies and deceits of their minds.

Those drunk with imperial power
have fallen from their arrogant thrones.
The dispossessed on the scrapheap
have been empowered one with another.

The homeless and the hungry
have been fed with their share of the harvest.
The greedy who hold on to their wealth
have seen it all crumble and vanish.

Just and compassionate God,
giving a new name to the deprived and invisible,
you fulfil your covenants of promise.
Long ago you gave Abraham your blessing,
and to Sarah, both faithful and true.

Your love reaches to every generation,
to the earth's little people, for ever.
Now is the blessing renewed:
I give you my heartfelt thanks
with eyes that are shining with love.

Gospel Acclamation

Alleluia, alleluia, alleluia.
Alleluia, alleluia, alleluia.

Keep awake. Be alert.
Open your eyes – look – and see!
Open your ears – listen – and hear!
Keep awake. Be alert.

THE FOURTH SUNDAY OF ADVENT

You do not know when the time will come.
Alleluia, alleluia, alleluia.

A reading from the Gospel according to Matthew/Mark/Luke
Alleluia, alleluia, alleluia.

A   Matthew 24.36–44
B   Mark 13.24–37
C   Luke 21.25–36

Give glory to the living God.
Alleluia, alleluia, alleluia.
Unfold the Living Word for us today.

Collects

Year A

Living Presence, yearning for us,
  voicing your promise
    in the music of the psalms,
    in the voice of the prophets,
    in the dreams of Joseph,
  embodying that promise in the womb of Mary,
inspire us to welcome Jesus, Emmanuel, God-with-us,
  and to embody his Spirit
    in our music,
    in our voices,
    in our lives,
that we may become
  the good news of your Commonwealth.
We pray this through the One
  in whose constant coming we trust,
  whose day is always near.

THE FOURTH SUNDAY OF ADVENT

Year B

Mysterious Presence,
  here in our midst,
  disclosing the secret
    hidden in the deep places of our hearts,
      for whom we wait,
      for whom we listen,
may we hear your voice
  and respond to your invitation,
and, like Mary, embrace your will,
  welcoming your incarnation in our flesh.
We pray this through the One
  in whose constant coming we trust,
  whose day is always near.

Year C

Unfathomable Mystery,
  in whom we live and move and have our being,
  of whose presence we are so often unaware,
may our hearts leap for joy
  in the silence of the approaching night,
  as your living Word becomes a human being,
  speaking to us through flesh and blood,
  through our neighbours, our enemies,
    and our friends.
We pray this through the One
  in whose constant coming we trust,
  whose day is always near.

THE FOURTH SUNDAY OF ADVENT

4

Mysterious Presence,
    moving among us in the darkness of these days,
        obscure, silent, unrecognized,
point us once more to a hidden birth,
    a newborn cry,
    and a home where at last we know that we belong.
We pray this in the Spirit of the One
    who was and is and always will be
        most at home in you.

5

Unknown One,
    announcing your presence
        not among the powerful but in obscurity,
overshadow us now,
    and speak to the hidden places of our being,
that, entering your darkness with joy,
    we may choose, with you,
    to bring new life to birth,
in the Spirit of the One whose coming we await,
    with expectant hearts and minds.

Christmas Eve
24 December
Years A, B, C

Kyries

You come to us in human flesh,
and we have wounded one another's bodies.

You come to us as a baby,
and we have wounded those who are vulnerable.

You come to us as an outcast,
and we have hardened our hearts.

Response/Canticle/Hymn/Reflection

The people who walked in darkness
have seen a great light;
those who dwelt in a land of deep darkness,
upon them has the light dawned.

As a child you have been born to us,
as a son you have been given to us:
Wonderful counsellor, Creator God,
Beloved Abba, harbinger of peace.

From the days of our ancestors of faith
in fulfilment of the covenants of promise,
your word of love has struggled to be born,
and at last is made clear in the word made flesh.

Gospel Acclamation

Alleluia, alleluia, alleluia.
Alleluia, alleluia, alleluia.
Hear the great words of the covenant,
justice and truth,
mercy and forgiveness,
freedom and courage,
compassion and loving kindness.
Alleluia, alleluia, alleluia.

A reading from the Gospel according to Luke
Alleluia, alleluia, alleluia.

Luke 1.67–79

Give glory to the living God.
Alleluia, alleluia, alleluia.
Unfold the Living Word for us today.

Collects

1

Living God, discerning and loving,
   wonderfully creating us in your image,
   striving with our reluctant wills
      to repair and restore us,
   renewing us in Jesus when we fail to love,
so fill us with your spirit
   that we may judge aright the way we ought to go,
   and be given strength faithfully to follow to the end.
We pray this in the Presence of the One
   who always comes to us as both Child and Judge.

2

Living One, present to Abraham and Sarah,
   to David and his descendants,
unwearied in your love for us
   and steadfast in your covenant,
wonderful beyond words
   in your gift to us of Jesus,
stir our hearts to an outpouring of gratitude,
   our thanksgiving that you take such delight in humanity,
and by this night's marriage of earth and heaven
   draw all generations into the embrace of your love.

Christmas Night
24–25 December
Years A, B, C

Kyries

You come to us in human flesh,
and we have wounded one another's bodies.

You come to us as a baby,
and we have wounded those who are vulnerable.

You come to us as an outcast,
and we have hardened our hearts.

Response/Canticle/Hymn/Reflection

From the days of our ancestors of faith,
in fulfilment of the covenants of promise,
your dream of love, dear God, is born,
alive for us in a baby's cry.

Gratitude that we belong to you for ever!
Gratitude for the power of love,
loosening the grip of evil,
transforming pain to joy,
swallowing death for ever.

Gratitude for the vulnerable baby.
**Gratitude for the weakness stronger than our strength,
bringer of solid joys and lasting treasure.**
Gratitude for the gifts of one another,
given that we may learn to bear the beams of love.

From the days of our ancestors of faith,
in fulfilment of the covenants of promise,
your dream of love, dear God, is born,
alive for us in a baby's cry.

Gospel Acclamation

Alleluia, alleluia, alleluia.
Alleluia, alleluia, alleluia.
Look for the glory of God
revealed in flesh and blood.
Alleluia, alleluia, alleluia.

A reading from the Gospel according to John
Alleluia, alleluia, alleluia.

John 1.1–14

Give glory to the living God.
Alleluia, alleluia, alleluia.
Unfold the Living Word for us today.

Collects

1

Living Presence, radiant with glory,
  giving us, on this most sacred night,
  the Gift we hardly knew was our deepest heart's desire,
draw us into the mystery of your love,
  bring us once more to the manger,
  a song of joy on our lips,
  a shining wonder in our eyes.
We pray this in the Spirit of Jesus, Word made flesh,
  in the splendour of eternal light, now and for ever.

2

Living Presence of the night as well as of the day,
  making the darkness both deepen and dazzle,
shine with the brightness of heavenly light,
illuminate and transform our faces,
  as you shone through the flesh and blood
    of a baby of this earth,
that we may trust and embody
  the vision of glory and bliss.
We pray this in the Spirit of the One
  whose birth we celebrate this silent night.

3

Living Spirit,
  whispering to us in the silence of the night,
  swelling our hearts to a strange rejoicing,
illuminate and warm us through the cold,
  that we may greet the Morning Star,
  and know that the dream will never fade.
We pray this in the living Presence of the One
  whose birth we celebrate this midnight hour.

Christmas Morning
25 December
Years A, B, C

Kyries

You come to us in human flesh,
and we have wounded one another's bodies.

You come to us as a baby,
and we have wounded those who are vulnerable.

You come to us as an outcast,
and we have hardened our hearts.

Response/Canticle/Hymn/Reflection

From the days of our ancestors of faith,
in fulfilment of the covenants of promise,
your dream of love, dear God, is born,
alive for us in a baby's cry.

Gratitude that we belong to you for ever!
Gratitude for the power of love,
loosening the grip of evil,
transforming pain to joy,
swallowing death for ever.

Gratitude for the vulnerable baby.
**Gratitude for the weakness stronger than our strength,
bringer of solid joys and lasting treasure.**
Gratitude for the gifts of one another,
given that we may learn to bear the beams of love.

From the days of our ancestors of faith,
in fulfilment of the covenants of promise,
your dream of love, dear God, is born,
alive for us in a baby's cry.

Gospel Acclamation

Alleluia, alleluia, alleluia.
Alleluia, alleluia, alleluia.
Listen with your hearts to the angels' song,
run gladly to the manger as did the shepherds,
ponder deep within you as a mother with a great mystery in her arms.
Alleluia, alleluia, alleluia.

A reading from the Gospel according to Luke
Alleluia, alleluia, alleluia.

Luke 2.1–14 [15–20]

Give glory to the living God.
Alleluia, alleluia, alleluia.
Unfold the Living Word for us today.

Collects

1

Living Presence, on this glad morning,
   dawning with loving kindness,
   shining upon us with tender compassion,
   revealing to us the gift of yourself
     in the infant Jesus,
fill us with wonder on this sacred day,
   awestruck by this treasure,
   vulnerable in our hands,
that our lives may embody your unconditional love.
We pray this in the Spirit of Jesus, Word made flesh,
   in the splendour of eternal life, now and for ever.

2

Living Presence, mothering, nurturing,
   opening our eyes to the wonder of the birth of a baby,
     unique and dearly loved,
may we, like Mary,
   treasure your Presence in flesh and blood,
   pondering these things in our hearts,
and, like the shepherds,
   may we give you praise and glory
   for all that we have heard and seen.
We pray this in the Spirit of Jesus, Word made flesh,
   in the splendour of eternal life, now and for ever.

Christmas Day
25 December
Years A, B, C

Kyries

You come to us in human flesh,
and we have wounded one another's bodies.

You come to us as a baby,
and we have wounded those who are vulnerable.

You come to us as an outcast,
and we have hardened our hearts.

Response/Canticle/Hymn/Reflection

From the days of our ancestors of faith,
in fulfilment of the covenants of promise,
your dream of love, dear God, is born,
alive for us in a baby's cry.

Gratitude that we belong to you for ever!
Gratitude for the power of love,
loosening the grip of evil,
transforming pain to joy,
swallowing death for ever.

Gratitude for the vulnerable baby.
**Gratitude for the weakness stronger than our strength,
bringer of solid joys and lasting treasure.**
Gratitude for the gifts of one another,
given that we may learn to bear the beams of love.

From the days of our ancestors of faith,
in fulfilment of the covenants of promise,
your dream of love, dear God, is born,
alive for us in a baby's cry.

Gospel Acclamation

Alleluia, alleluia, alleluia.
Alleluia, alleluia, alleluia.
Look for the glory of God
revealed in flesh and blood.
Alleluia, alleluia, alleluia.

A reading from the Gospel according to Luke
Alleluia, alleluia, alleluia.

Luke 2.1–7[8–20]

Give glory to the living God.
Alleluia, alleluia, alleluia.
Unfold the Living Word for us today.

Collect

Living Presence of grace,
  bringing glad tidings of peace
  and good news of liberation,
may radiance and bliss
  shine through the faces of all who celebrate his birth,
that the light that no darkness can extinguish
  may grow stronger in the benighted places of the world.
We pray this in the Spirit of Jesus, Word made flesh,
  in the splendour of eternal light, now and for ever.

The First Sunday of Christmas
Years A, B, C

Kyries

You come to us in human flesh,
and we have wounded one another's bodies.

You come to us as a baby,
and we have wounded those who are vulnerable.

You come to us as an outcast,
and we have hardened our hearts.

Response/Canticle/Hymn/Reflection

Eternal Word of the living God,
dream from before the beginning,
in whom and through whom everything has come to be,
in you is life, the life that is our light,
the light that shines on in the darkness,
which the darkness has never overcome,
the true light, enlightening humanity,
shining in the world.

Yet we did not recognize you.
You came to your own people –
and we did not know you.

THE FIRST SUNDAY OF CHRISTMAS

You came to your own home –
and we did not receive you.

But to those who heard a whisper of the Word,
who were stirred to life by the dream,
to those who believed in your mysterious name,
you gave power to become your children,
to be known as your servants and your friends,
who were born, not of the desire and will of our flesh,
but of the desire and will of your love.

Living Word of light and love,
you became a human being,
and lived the fullness of our humanity,
full of grace and truth.

We saw your glory,
divine glory shining through a human face,
as a mother's eyes live through her daughter's,
as a son reflects his father's image,
your glory in a human being fully alive.

Gospel Acclamation

Alleluia, alleluia, alleluia.
Alleluia, alleluia, alleluia.

A Hear the call out of slavery and exile,
    claim your freedom and your true home.
B Treasure these words;
    ponder them in your heart.
C Ponder in your hearts the words of wisdom.

Alleluia, alleluia, alleluia.

THE FIRST SUNDAY OF CHRISTMAS

A reading from the Gospel according to Matthew/Luke
Alleluia, alleluia, alleluia.

A   Matthew 2.13–23
B   Luke 2.15–21
C   Luke 2.41–52

Give glory to the living God.
Alleluia, alleluia, alleluia.
Unfold the Living Word for us today.

Collects

Year A

Loving Presence,
   companion of all who flee for their lives,
open our hearts in generous welcome
   to the bewildered and frightened,
that in friendship with them
   we may find a healing home
      for our own hurt child from long ago.
We pray this in the Spirit of Jesus, Word made flesh,
   in the splendour of eternal light, now and for ever.

Year B

Living Presence,
   cradling us at the beginning of our lives,
   embracing us at journey's end,
   loving us as your own,
bind us together, families and friends,
that, as the Child in Nazareth,
   we may grow in wisdom and maturity,
   followers of your living word.
We pray this in the Spirit of Jesus, Word made flesh,
   in the splendour of eternal light, now and for ever.

THE FIRST SUNDAY OF CHRISTMAS

Year C

Living Presence, moving among us,
    adopting us as daughters and sons,
    calling us and uniting us by your living word,
as we ponder the mystery of Nazareth
    may we find in you the source of our worth,
    direction for our lives,
    and the unity of our families and communities.
We pray this in the Spirit of Jesus, Word made flesh,
    in the splendour of eternal light, now and for ever.

The Second Sunday of Christmas
Years A, B, C

Kyries

You come to us in human flesh,
and we have wounded one another's bodies.

You come to us as a baby,
and we have wounded those who are vulnerable.

You come to us as an outcast,
and we have hardened our hearts.

Response/Canticle/Hymn/Reflection

Thanksgiving

Eternal One, always alive,
unconditionally loving, giver of all good gifts,
your lovingkindness warms us again,
and our hearts overflow with gratitude.
You are creating us, making us,
you are repairing us, restoring us.
You nourish us with the means of grace,
you renew in us the hope of glory.
We respond with thankfulness
and give ourselves to your service.

Let us walk with you in compassion,
and thirst with you for justice.

The first Sunday in the new year

Christ has no body now on earth
but yours and mine this day,
to serve with tact the common good,
to suffer and to pray.

Ours are the eyes through which Christ sees,
compassionate, piercing, clear,
ours are the mouths through which Christ speaks
of love that melts all fear.

Ours are the ears, attentive, quiet,
through which Christ listens much,
and Christ now works with healing power
through hands that reach and touch.

We promise as a new year dawns
to live each moment well,
to serve and listen, touch and heal,
the greatest story tell,

with Christ-likeness, incarnate, now
one human race on earth,
gifts to each other, still unpacked,
of wonder and of worth.

THE SECOND SUNDAY OF CHRISTMAS

Gospel Acclamation

Alleluia, alleluia, alleluia.
Alleluia, alleluia, alleluia.
Listen for the Word in the very marrow of your being.
Alleluia, alleluia, alleluia.

A reading from the Gospel according to John
Alleluia, alleluia, alleluia.

John 1.[1–9] 10–18

Give glory to the living God.
Alleluia, alleluia, alleluia.
Unfold the Living Word for us today.

Collect

Abiding Presence,
   dwelling among us that we might dwell with you,
awaken us to the hope that is in us,
   and to the glory that is our destiny,
to which, with the whole creation,
     we are being called and lured.
We pray this in the Spirit of Jesus, Word made flesh,
   Dream incarnate, hope of the world.

Collects for Weekdays during the Christmas Season, until the Saturday after the Feast of the Epiphany

1

Living Presence, loving from all eternity,
   born of a woman's body,
   dwelling among us
      that we might look upon you
      and touch you with our own hands,
may we so cherish one another in our bodies
   that we realize that we have been touched by you.
We pray this in the Spirit of Jesus,
   divine creative Word made flesh.

2

Living Presence, radiant with glory,
   giving us the Gift we hardly knew was our deepest heart's desire,
draw us into the mystery of your love,
   bring us once more to the manger,
   a song of joy on our lips,
   a shining wonder in our eyes.
We pray this in the Spirit of Jesus, Word made flesh,
   in the splendour of eternal light, now and for ever.

3

Living Presence in the morning,
  dawning with loving kindness,
  shining upon us with tender compassion,
  revealing to us the gift of yourself
    in the infant Jesus,
fill us with wonder at this sacred time,
  awestruck by this treasure,
  vulnerable in our hands,
that our lives may embody your unconditional love.
We pray this in the Spirit of Jesus, Word made flesh,
  in the splendour of eternal light, now and for ever.

4

Living Presence, mothering, nurturing,
  opening our eyes to the wonder of a birth of a baby,
    unique and dearly loved,
may we, like Mary,
  treasure your Presence in flesh and blood,
  pondering these things in our hearts,
and, like the shepherds,
  may we give you praise and glory
  for all that we have heard and seen.
We pray this in the Spirit of Jesus, Word made flesh,
  in the splendour of eternal light, now and for ever.

5

Living Presence of grace,
   bringing glad tidings of peace
   and good news of liberation,
may radiance and bliss
   shine through the faces of all who celebrate his birth,
that the light that no darkness can extinguish
   may grow stronger in the benighted places of the world.
We pray this in the Spirit of Jesus, Word made flesh,
   in the splendour of eternal light, now and for ever.

6

Living Presence of unbounded love,
   revealed among us as a human being,
   at home in flesh and blood,
give us delight in one another,
   our bodies a means of your grace,
   our newborn a reminder of your love,
   and our faces the image of your glory.
We pray this in the Spirit of Jesus, Word made flesh,
   in the splendour of eternal light, now and for ever.

7

Living Presence, moving among us,
   adopting us as daughters and sons,
   calling us and uniting us by your living word,
as we ponder the mystery of Nazareth
   may we find in you the source of our worth,
   direction for our lives,
   and the unity of our families and communities.
We pray this in the Spirit of Jesus, Word made flesh,
   in the splendour of eternal light, now and for ever.

8 (Years B and C)

Loving Presence,
> companion of all who flee for their lives,
open our hearts in generous welcome
> to the bewildered and frightened,
that in friendship with them
> we may find a healing home
>> for our own hurt child from long ago.
We pray this in the Spirit of Jesus, Word made flesh,
> in the splendour of eternal light, now and for ever.

9 (Years A and C)

Living Presence,
> cradling us at the beginning of our lives,
> embracing us at journey's end,
> loving us as your own,
bind us together, families and friends,
that, as the Child in Nazareth,
> we may grow in wisdom and maturity,
> followers of your living word.
We pray this in the Spirit of Jesus, Word made flesh,
> in the splendour of eternal light, now and for ever.

10 (Years A and B)

Living Presence, moving among us,
> adopting us as daughters and sons,
> calling us and uniting us by your living word,
as we ponder the mystery of Nazareth
> may we find in you the source of our worth,
> direction for our lives,
> and the unity of our families and communities.
We pray this in the Spirit of Jesus, Word made flesh,
> in the splendour of eternal light, now and for ever.

The Epiphany
6 January
Years A, B, C

Kyries

We have preferred those who are glamorous and clever;
we have not listened to those who are hidden and wise.

We have let our passions drown the still small voice of truth.

We have argued with others and not listened to their stories.

Response/Canticle/Hymn/Reflection

The grace of God has appeared
for the salvation of all people.
Lift up your eyes, cities of God, and see:
**people of all lands coming together,
greeting one another from all over the world.**

So you will know and be glad,
your heart will thrill and rejoice.
Arise, shine, Jerusalem, for your light has come,
and the glory of God has risen upon you.

Glory to God in the highest, alleluia!
On earth peace to people of goodwill, alleluia!

All the ends of the earth have seen
the salvation of our God: alleluia!

Gospel Acclamation

Alleluia, alleluia, alleluia.
Alleluia, alleluia, alleluia.
Being warned by God in a dream
they returned to their own country another way.
Alleluia, alleluia, alleluia.

A reading from the Gospel according to Matthew
Alleluia, alleluia, alleluia.

Matthew 2.1–12

Give glory to the living God.
Alleluia, alleluia, alleluia.
Unfold the Living Word for us today.

Collect

Living Presence of glory,
   your star rising in splendour,
   your radiance in the eyes of the Child
     piercing the darkness of our slumber,
     signalling the dawn of a new commonwealth
      of peace and justice,
enlighten us when we are tempted
   to fall back into gloom,
beckon the nations to your light,
and guide all humanity to your glory.
We pray this in the Spirit of Jesus,
   Word made flesh,
   Dream incarnate,
   Hope of the world.

The First Sunday of Epiphany
The Baptism of Christ

Kyries

We have not always kept the promises we once made to one another and to God.

We have let others down by what we have failed to do.

We have, in half-remembered ways, added to the burden of the gonewrongness of the world.

Response/Canticle/Hymn/Reflection

The lights of the city shine in the darkness,
extending the day into winter's night.
The lamps in the streets guide the traveller,
the lights in the houses bid welcome.

Let the cities of God's commonwealth rejoice,
the light of the world reflected in their window panes.
Let the people gather at festival times,
to give thanks in the cities of peace.

THE FIRST SUNDAY OF EPIPHANY

For the light and glory of God have come,
illuminating the darkest of alleyways,
enlightening the darkest of hearts and minds,
giving wisdom to those in authority.
In the light of Christ all strife will shrivel away,
the sounds of violence no longer heard in their streets.
The doors of hospitality will be open,
the stranger given welcome and lodging.

The sun will no longer be their light by day,
nor will the moon give light to them by night.
For God will be their everlasting light,
and their God will be their glory.

Gospel Acclamation

Alleluia, alleluia, alleluia.
Alleluia, alleluia, alleluia.

Hear the voice from the cloud of the Presence:
You are my beloved in whom I take great delight.
Alleluia, alleluia, alleluia.

A reading from the Gospel according to Matthew/Mark/Luke
Alleluia, alleluia, alleluia.

A   *Matthew 3.13–17*
B   *Mark 1.4–11*
C   *Luke 3.15–17,21–22*

Give glory to the living God.
Alleluia, alleluia, alleluia.
Unfold the Living Word for us today.

THE FIRST SUNDAY OF EPIPHANY

Collects

Year A

Living Presence of promise and of covenant,
anointing Jesus with the power of the Holy Spirit
   to be a light to the nations
   and a liberator to the captives,
so empower your people
   that we may proclaim with our lips
      the good news of your freedom,
   and show forth in our lives
      the patterns of your justice.
We pray this in the Spirit of the living Jesus,
   embraced for ever in your glory.

Year B

Liberating Presence,
   calling your people in faith
      to cross the River Jordan,
   challenging the powers that oppress
      in every generation,
   empowering Jesus to embody the way of justice,
so enable us in your Holy Spirit,
   that we may touch one another
      with the gift of water that makes us one,
      equal in dignity and worth,
      sisters and brothers in the new community
         of all who recognize in you
            the source of true liberation.
We pray this in the Spirit of the living Jesus,
   embraced for ever in your glory.

THE FIRST SUNDAY OF EPIPHANY

Year C

Living Presence at our beginnings,
    affirming in the baptism of Jesus
        that he belonged to you
        and that you delighted in him,
so reassure us
    that through the waters of our birth and baptism
        we dwell in you,
and that as sons and daughters in your Spirit,
    you rejoice in us.
We pray this in the Spirit of the living Jesus,
    embraced for ever in your glory.

4

Mysterious Presence,
    whose beauty is beyond our imagining,
    and whose power we cannot comprehend,
show us your glory
    as bright as we dare contemplate it,
and shield us from seeing more than we can bear,
until the day dawns when we can look upon you without fear.
We pray this in the Spirit of the One
    whose eyes pierce like laser beams,
    and whose face shines with your light.

5

Living Presence of roaring fire and kindly flame,
    seeking to harness the wild winds of our winter,
    burning the decayed and warming new seeds,
steady our hearts and deepen our trust,
and lead us through the deaththroes of the old age
    and the birthpangs of the new.
We pray this after the pattern of Jesus
    and in the power of the Spirit.

6

Living Presence, stirring Abraham,
    and moving among all humanity,
  whose justice transforms our divisions,
  whose love puts our words and customs
    in their place,
draw the peoples of faith closer together,
  ancient and ever new,
that we may care deeply for one another,
  and worship you in this our day
    in spirit and in truth.
We pray this after the pattern of Jesus
  and in the power of the Spirit.

The Second Sunday of Epiphany

Kyries

We have been blinded by greed.

We have let envy embitter us.

We have not opened our hearts and pockets in generosity.

Response/Canticle/Hymn/Reflection

Arise, shine, for your light has come,
and the glory of God is shining upon you,
even though darkest night still covers the earth,
and thick darkness the peoples.
The city has no need of sun or moon to shine upon it,
for the glory of God is its light,
and its lamp is the human one,
    shining and transfigured.

God will arise upon you like the dawn,
and God's glory will be seen in your midst.
Nations shall come to your light,
rulers to the brightness of your rising.
The city has no need of sun or moon to shine upon it,
for the glory of God is its light,
and its lamp is the human one,
    shining and transfigured.

THE SECOND SUNDAY OF EPIPHANY

The sun will no more be your light by day,
nor will the moon give light to you by night,
for God will be your everlasting light,
and your God will be your glory.
The city has no need of sun or moon to shine upon it,
for the glory of God is its light,
and its lamp is the human one,
   shining and transfigured.

Gospel Acclamation

Alleluia, alleluia, alleluia.
Alleluia, alleluia, alleluia.

A & B   Listen to the call, Follow me.
C   Be transformed by the riches of God's grace.

Alleluia, alleluia, alleluia.

A reading from the Gospel according to John
Alleluia, alleluia, alleluia.

A   *John 1.29–42*
B   *John 1.43–51*
C   *John 2.1–11*

Give glory to the living God.
Alleluia, alleluia, alleluia.
Unfold the Living Word for us today.

Collects

Year A

Living Presence,
    calling us to give what we most treasure in your service,
    as you called your Beloved
        to reveal your glory to humankind,
give us courage to respond to your invitation,
    wholeheartedly and without reserve,
and give us good cheer to help us on the Way.
We pray this in the Spirit of the living Jesus,
    embraced for ever in your glory.

Year B

Living Presence,
    calling us before we were given a name,
tune our ears that we may be attentive to your voice,
    and our whole being eager to respond,
that, having discovered you in Jesus,
    we may draw others
        to listen,
        to awaken,
        and to become followers of the Way.
We pray this in the Spirit of the living Jesus,
    embraced for ever in your glory.

THE SECOND SUNDAY OF EPIPHANY

Year C

Living Presence,
   of rejoicing and enjoyment,
      companion at the wedding feast,
give us the spirit of grateful delight
   in the gifts you have given us,
and give us the spirit of generosity
   to take pleasure in the gifts you have given to others.
We pray this in the Spirit of the living Jesus,
   embraced for ever in your glory.

4

Living Presence,
   Light of the universe,
   revealed to us as utter and unfailing love,
   in Jesus of Nazareth, a man and a Jew,
draw us to yourself as you have drawn so many,
   men and women,
   Jews and Gentiles,
   shepherds and wise men,
   nomads and settlers,
that human beings may embrace one another,
   and the whole world at last reflect your glory.

THE SECOND SUNDAY OF EPIPHANY

5

Living Presence,
    challenging us with the truths the human heart resists,
    embodying them in Jesus,
give us courage to listen to him,
    as to the prophets in our own country,
        who show the light
            that we do not wish to see,
        who point to strangers
            as revealers of unwelcome truth,
        who challenge us to take the risks
            we would prefer to avoid.
We pray this in the Spirit of the only One
    whose light awakens us,
    whose warmth encourages us,
    and whose vision empowers us to act.

6

Compassionate Presence to the rejected and the lost,
    embracing the outcast and the exile,
    within us or beyond our gates,
may those who are fortunate open wide their doors
    to welcome home those who have fallen by the way,
and may the weary not begrudge the contentment
        of the simple blessings of home,
where, in quiet ways,
    sorrows are eased and envy is dispelled.
We pray this in the Spirit of Jesus,
    courteous and hospitable to all.

The Third Sunday of Epiphany

Kyries

We have not put the voice of the voiceless first.

We have colluded with the structures of greed.

We have put money first, loving it too much.

Response/Canticle/Hymn/Reflection

A hymn to Wisdom

Holy Wisdom, delight of our God,
you open our ears, we hear your word.
You enter deep into the being of humanity;
foolish to the world, you unmask our follies.
You are a shelter to us by day,
and a steady flame through the night.
You lead us through turbulent waters,
and bring us safe to dry ground.
Holy Wisdom, delight of our God,
you open our ears, we hear your word.
You open the mouths of those who are mute,
you loosen the tongues of infants in their cries.
A little child takes us by the hand,
and leads us to freedom and truth.

THE THIRD SUNDAY OF EPIPHANY

Holy Wisdom, delight of our God,
you open our ears, we hear your word.

Gospel Acclamation

Alleluia, alleluia, alleluia.
Alleluia, alleluia, alleluia.

A Listen to the call, Follow me.
B Be transformed by the riches of God's grace.
C Listen for wind of the Spirit, whose power gives flesh and blood to these ancient words.

Alleluia, alleluia, alleluia.

A reading from the Gospel according to Matthew/John/Luke
Alleluia, alleluia, alleluia.

A *Matthew 4.12–23*
B *John 2.1–11*
C *Luke 4.14–21*

Alleluia, alleluia, alleluia.

Give glory to the living God.
Alleluia, alleluia, alleluia.
Unfold the Living Word for us today.

THE THIRD SUNDAY OF EPIPHANY

Collects

Year A

Living Presence of glory,
  whose splendour dazzles the darkness of this world,
give us courage to follow Jesus,
    the True Human Being,
  into the dark places of our hearts,
that, with all humankind,
  we may be enlightened and transformed.
We pray this in the Spirit of the living Jesus,
  embraced for ever in your glory.

Year B

Living Presence of mysterious and hidden power,
    stirring to life the waters of creation,
    yet receiving the cup of water we offer one another,
transform such simple deeds
    into the wine of the new creation,
surprising us with a joy beyond all expectation.
We pray this in the Spirit of the living Jesus,
    embraced for ever in your glory.

Year C

Living Presence of compassion,
    embracing us at the point of our greatest need,
    implanting in our hearts the law of wisdom, justice, and
        mercy,
fulfil in us and in all humankind your promises,
that we may receive, embody, and proclaim them
    in the wide open spaces of your freedom.
We pray this in the Spirit of the living Jesus,
    embraced for ever in your glory.

THE THIRD SUNDAY OF EPIPHANY

4

Living Presence of love,
    revealed among us as a human being,
    at home in flesh and blood,
give us delight in one another,
    our bodies a means of your grace,
    our newborn a reminder of your love,
    and our faces the image of your glory.
We pray this in the Spirit of Jesus, Word made flesh,
    in the splendour of eternal light, now and for ever.

5

Constant Presence,
    enduring in love through every passing age,
    bearing the long nights of darkness in your heart,
bring us at the last to see the morning star,
    be born again in us
        at the breaking of the day,
    and come to abundant life in us
        in the glory of the noonday sun.
We pray this in the name of the One
    who shines among us as the light of the world.

6

Pioneer of the living way,
    whose cloud and fire goes on before us,
give us courage to traverse the waste and barren places,
    trusting that we shall come at last
        to our true home,
        to the gardens of harmony,
        and to the cities of justice.
We pray this after the pattern of Jesus
    and in the power of the Spirit.

The Fourth Sunday of Epiphany

Kyries

We have not given enough time to listen to others who are different from ourselves.

We have refused the cost of the way of dialogue,
and we have made others pay the cost of conflict.

We have colluded with persecutions and inquisitions,
and we have refused to take to heart and mind the truths that others have discerned.

Response/Canticle/Hymn/Reflection

Gratitude for the love that accepts us whatever!
Gratitude for the love that floods our inmost hearts!

Gratitude for the love that brings peace out of strife!
Gratitude for the love that floods our inmost hearts!

Gratitude for the love that loosens the grip of evil!
Gratitude for the love that floods our inmost hearts!

Gratitude for the love that binds us together for ever!
Gratitude for the love that floods our inmost hearts!

THE FOURTH SUNDAY OF EPIPHANY

Gratitude for the love that never ceases to forgive!
Gratitude for the love that floods our inmost hearts!

Gratitude for the love that enfolds with gentleness!
Gratitude for the love that floods our inmost hearts!

Gratitude for the love that endures the suffering!
Gratitude for the love that floods our inmost hearts!

Gratitude for the love that trusts that Nothing shall be All!

Gospel Acclamation

Alleluia, alleluia, alleluia.
Alleluia, alleluia, alleluia.

A   Be transformed by the riches of God's grace.
B   Be alert to the words and deeds of transforming power.
C   Listen for the Word that pierces to the heart and gives light to the mind.

Alleluia, alleluia, alleluia.

A reading from the Gospel according to John/Mark/Luke
Alleluia, alleluia, alleluia.

A   *John 2.1–11*
B   *Mark 1.21–28*
C   *Luke 2.22–40*

Give glory to the living God.
Alleluia, alleluia, alleluia.
Unfold the Living Word for us today.

THE FOURTH SUNDAY OF EPIPHANY

Collects

Year A

Living Presence, overflowing with generosity,
    taking the little that we offer,
        of meal and oil,
        of bread and fish,
        of water and wine,
    blessing them with thankfulness,
open our hearts with the spirit of generosity,
    that we may distribute among us all
    everything we are no longer tempted to hoard,
    and so fulfil your desire
        for your justice to abound on earth.
We pray this in the Spirit of the living Jesus,
    embraced for ever in your glory.

Year B

Holy Presence,
    speaking with authority through Jesus,
        his words and actions seamlessly one,
bring into harmony all that we say and do,
that evil may not be on the loose in us,
    and that we may know your power to heal and save.
We pray this in the Spirit of the living Jesus,
    embraced for ever in your glory.

Year C

Living Presence of light and glory,
    shining through the faces of the watchful who waited
        through the years,
    and through the face of the infant young in days,

enlighten us with grace and wisdom,
    that we may mature into the innocence
        that no longer even desires to harm.
We pray this in the Spirit of the living Jesus,
    embraced for ever in your glory.

4

Living Presence of bliss and wonder,
    surprising us beyond all that we could imagine,
release in us a deep and rumbling laughter,
that from our bellies may flow the ripples of joy,
    the living water that makes the desert bloom,
    and the true of heart delight in one another's love.
We pray this in the Spirit of the living Jesus,
    embraced for ever in your glory.

5

Living Presence, disturbing and liberating,
    whose speech is pregnant with power,
    and whose word itself is deed,
keep us dissatisfied with all that distorts your truth,
and make our hearts attentive to your liberating voice in Jesus
    Christ,
    your Word made flesh,
        made lungs and lips and tongue and larynx,
    whose words are carried on the wind
        to awaken the very cells of our being.
We pray indeed in that Spirit,
    the Spirit of the One
        who lived the truth that sets us free.

The Feast of the Presentation of Christ in the Temple
2 February

Kyries

We are addicted to power.

We wallow in popularity.

We are deceived by prestige.

Response/Canticle/Hymn/Reflection

We give you thanks, Beloved,
we have lived to see this day.
Your promise is fulfilled,
and our duty done.
Each night you give us your peace,
for we have glimpsed with our own eyes
the liberation you prepare for all people,
a light to the world in its darkness,
and the glory of all who serve your love.

THE PRESENTATION OF CHRIST IN THE TEMPLE

Gospel Acclamation

Alleluia, alleluia, alleluia.
Alleluia, alleluia, alleluia.
Listen for the Word that pierces to the heart
and gives light to the mind.
Alleluia, alleluia, alleluia.

A reading from the Gospel according to Luke
Alleluia, alleluia, alleluia.

Luke 2.22–40

Give glory to the living God.
Alleluia, alleluia, alleluia.
Unfold the Living Word for us today.

Collect

Living Presence of searing light,
   laying bare our inmost thoughts,
   piercing our hearts with a laser,
purify and enlighten us,
   that we may mature into wisdom,
   and grow to our full stature in your grace.
We pray this in the Spirit of the living Jesus,
   embraced for ever in your glory.

If further Collects are needed for weekdays after 2 February those for the week after the Fourth Sunday of Epiphany may be used.

The Fifth Sunday before Lent

Kyries

We have not brought zest to the life of others.

We have not brought light to dark places.

We have not risked a healing touch.

Response/Canticle/Hymn/Reflection

Seven sins to seven virtues

Puncture our bloated pride:
sow the hidden seed of humility.
Root out our cruel and bitter anger:
sow the hidden seed of courtesy.
Disentangle us from the web of envy:
sow the hidden seed of justice.
Make clear the hypocrisies of our lust:
sow the hidden seed of truth.
Ease our grip from money:
sow the hidden seed of generosity.
Still our gluttonous pursuit of pleasure:
sow the hidden seed of charity.
Penetrate the fog of our sloth:
sow the hidden seed of laughter.

THE FIFTH SUNDAY BEFORE LENT

Gospel Acclamation

Alleluia, alleluia, alleluia.
Alleluia, alleluia, alleluia.

A   Listen for the challenge to be both salt and light.
B   Take us by the hand and lift us up.
C   Launch out into the deep and let down your nets for a catch.

Alleluia, alleluia, alleluia.

A reading from the Gospel according to Matthew/Mark/Luke
Alleluia, alleluia, alleluia.

A   *Matthew 5.13–20*
B   *Mark 1. 29–39*
C   *Luke 5.1–11*

Give glory to the living God.
Alleluia, alleluia, alleluia.
Unfold the Living Word for us today.

Collects

Year A

Open-hearted Presence,
calling us to be as salt and light,
yet warning us not to think of ourselves
    holier than others or superior to them,
enable us to be still in their presence,
    stranger or child, enemy or friend,
    to welcome them with our eyes,

and to give them our attention,
not with condemnation but with compassion,
not with hatred but with love.
We pray this in the Spirit of the universal Christ,
alive in you for ever.

Year B

Compassionate Presence,
   aflame with yearning,
   alive in Jesus to heal by word and touch,
empower us in the Spirit
   to bring words of kindness to the broken-hearted,
   and a touch of calm to the fevered,
that together we may be made whole,
   raised to life in the power of your love.
We pray this in the Spirit of the universal Christ,
   incarnate and glorified,
   humanity alive in you for ever.

Year C

Living Presence, foolish in worldly eyes,
   pressing us to be the same
      in the sight of those around us,
invite us to let down our nets
   where we are sure there are no fish,
and to see your light in the eyes of those
   in whom we least expect to see you.
We pray this in the Spirit of the universal Christ,
   incarnate and glorified,
   humanity alive in you for ever.

THE FIFTH SUNDAY BEFORE LENT

4

Holy, loving Presence,
   in whom we live and move and have our being,
   making us for yourself
      so that our hearts are restless
      until they find their rest in you,
draw us to your service and friendship
   that we may find in you our perfect freedom
      and our lasting peace.
We pray this in the power of the Spirit
   and in the name of Jesus Christ.

5

Living Presence of wisdom,
   folly to all that is clever and worldly in us,
   yet never absent even in our darkness,
turn us upside down and inside out
   that we may see with new eyes
   and hear with new ears,
and in your light be enlightened with your truth.
We pray this in the power of the Spirit
   and in the name of Jesus Christ.

6

Living Presence, wise and discerning,
   whose eyes pierce with clarity and understanding,
show us the way,
   not of being blameless but of being forgiven,
   not of being successful but of being faithful,
   not of being perfect but of persevering,
accepted and embraced in the Spirit of the One
   who embodied your wisdom
   and showed us the cost of your love.

The Fourth Sunday before Lent

Kyries

We have drawn back from others through fear.

We have not risked a comforting hand on a shoulder.

We have flinched from letting others touch us.

Response/Canticle/Hymn/Reflection

Well-being and Woe: Beatitudes in the spirit of Luke

We are blessed if we are destitute and homeless:
we are not to be blamed;
we are already in God's domain.

We are blessed if we are starving and have to beg for food:
we are not at fault;
we shall be satisfied.

We are blessed if we are downtrodden and gaunt with grief:
we are not guilty;
we shall laugh for joy.

We are blessed if we are despised, persecuted, mocked, stigmatized:
we are not to be ashamed;

THE FOURTH SUNDAY BEFORE LENT

we are well loved,
and we shall be honoured.

Alas for the wealthy
with their contempt for the poor.
Alas for the overfed
with their hardness of heart.
Alas for the sleek
with their mocking scorn.
Alas for the successful
with their arrogant disdain.

Isolated, proud, frozen,
we cannot give true love;
we have not known it:
we do not know how to receive it.
We can be rescued only by you –
the ones we have rejected.
You hold us steadily with your eyes,
with the gaze of justice and compassion.
Will we draw from you the courage to fall into your arms
stretched forward in mercy to embrace us?

Gospel Acclamation

Alleluia, alleluia, alleluia.
Alleluia, alleluia, alleluia.

A Let your word be a simple Yes or No.
B Stretch out your hand to touch and heal.
C Listen to what is blighted and what is blessed.

Alleluia, alleluia, alleluia.

A reading from the Gospel according to Matthew/Mark/Luke
Alleluia, alleluia, alleluia.

THE FOURTH SUNDAY BEFORE LENT

A   Matthew 5.21–37
B   Mark 1.40–45
C   Luke 6.17–26

Give glory to the living God.
Alleluia, alleluia, alleluia.
Unfold the Living Word for us today.

Collects

Year A

Living Presence of discerning judgement,
   aware of all that is hidden within us,
sear your law of love into our hearts,
that our desires may be as gold refined in the fire,
that the energy of our anger may be channelled
   into striving for justice,
and that our wills may be strengthened
   to endure the costly way of reconciliation.
We pray this in the Spirit of the universal Christ,
   incarnate and glorified,
     humanity alive in you for ever.

Year B

Living Presence of compassion and justice,
   empowering Jesus to cure disease
     by word and touch,
   and to heal divisions
     by embracing the outcast and the stigmatized,

take from us all prejudice and fear,
and inspire us with courage
    that we may enjoy the company
        of the despised and the rejected
    and know that we belong together in your domain.
We pray this in the Spirit of the universal Christ,
    incarnate and glorified,
    humanity alive in you for ever.

Year C

Living Presence of blight and blessing,
    of searing laser and compassionate eye,
judge us through the ones we pass by,
    stop us in our tracks,
    give us courage to draw near,
    and heal us with their embrace.
We pray this in the Spirit of the universal Christ,
    incarnate and glorified,
    humanity alive in you for ever.

4

Ever-creating Presence,
    ceaselessly at work
        through the groaning of the universe,
transform the body of this earth,
    that it might shine with your glory,
        reflected in the wounds of the Crucified and Risen One,
        in whose Spirit we pray.

THE FOURTH SUNDAY BEFORE LENT

5

Living Presence,
  calling human beings by thunder or by whisper
    to tread paths we feared
    and to make paths that have not yet been made,
guide us to find or pioneer our places
  within the patterns of service
  and the mosaics of ministry,
that we may embody your spirit of sacrificial love,
  proving to be faithful and true,
  and overcoming our fear of failure.
We pray this in the Spirit of the Crucified and Risen One,
  for whom all seemed lost,
  yet in whom all is being restored.

6

Living Presence, mysterious and wise,
  foolishness in clever worldly eyes,
surprise us at our wits' end,
  overturn our settled ways,
  open our eyes to the Crucified One,
that, knowing your last word is laughter,
  and realizing that emperors have no clothes,
we may take courage in speaking truth to power.
We pray this in the Spirit of Jesus,
  Clown of clowns and Fool of fools.

The Third Sunday before Lent

Kyries

We have been frozen by fear.

We have been paralysed by terror.

We have been stunned by violence.

Response/Canticle/Hymn/Reflection

Fools for Christ's sake

In facing the truth
may we be set free from delusion.
In accepting our wounds
may we be healed if not cured.
In embracing the outcast
may we know ourselves redeemed.
In discovering our inner child
may we grow to full stature.
In seeking true innocence
may we no longer harm.
In yielding to dying
may abundant life flow through us.
In vulnerable risk
may we know love's pain and joy.

In the release of laughter
may we hear the chuckle of God.
In the folly of the Cross
may we see the wisdom of God.

Gospel Acclamation

Alleluia, alleluia, alleluia.
Alleluia, alleluia, alleluia.

A & C Love your enemies. Pray for those who harass you.
B   Your sins are forgiven: Stand up and walk.

Alleluia, alleluia, alleluia.

A reading from the Gospel according to Matthew/Mark/Luke
Alleluia, alleluia, alleluia.

A *Matthew 5.38–48*
B *Mark 2.1–12*
C *Luke 6.27–38*

Give glory to the living God.
Alleluia, alleluia, alleluia.
Unfold the Living Word for us today.

Collects

Year A

Living Presence to the unnoticed and forgotten,
   embodying your love in the poor man of Nazareth,
keep alive in us the hope
   that the steady strength
     of the gentle and merciful

will overcome the brittle force
   of the fearful and powerful,
that those who are unrecognized
   will indeed inherit the earth.
We pray this after the pattern of Jesus
   and in the power of the Spirit.

Year B

Loving Presence,
   whose healing and forgiving power
      frees us from our paralysis
      and binds us together as one,
so empower us in your Spirit
   that we may discover that we can do as Jesus did,
   even that greater things are possible to us.
We pray this in the Spirit of the universal Christ,
   incarnate and glorified,
      humanity alive in you for ever.

Year C

Loving Presence,
   resisting evil by absorbing and dissolving it,
take from us all desire to harm
   and all thirst for revenge,
lift us off the spiral of violence,
give us courage to treat those who trouble us
   as equals to us in dignity and worth,
and strengthen our wills
   to build together a community that is just.
We pray this in the Spirit of the universal Christ,
   incarnate and glorified,
      humanity alive in you for ever.

THE THIRD SUNDAY BEFORE LENT

4

Living Presence,
   hidden among us as a nobody and a slave,
   refusing the panoplies of power,
so fill us with your Spirit
   that we may share your love in all sincerity,
   and come to know the wisdom
      of your wise and gentle rule.
We pray this in the Spirit that leads us
   to embrace the Way of Jesus.

5

Living Presence, healing and restoring,
   whose mercy is like a refining fire,
touch us with your judgement
   and confront us with your tenderness,
that, being sobered and comforted by you,
   we may reach out to those who are troubled,
that we may enfold even the planet in our arms,
and that we may hear the beating of your sacred heart.
We pray this through the One
   in whose constant coming we trust,
   whose day is always near.

6

Living Presence of the promise
    to Abraham and Sarah,
   blessing all their descendants in faith,
take from us our fear of the stranger,
   and hasten the gathering of all humanity
     in the city of peace,
      the dwelling place of all who love you.
We pray this in the Spirit of the One
   who was crucified outside Jerusalem.

The Second Sunday before Lent

Kyries

We have forgotten how dependent we are on what the oceans and earth give us.

We have used the earth for profit and not cherished it for food.

We have not exercised our knowledge of the earth wisely.

Response/Canticle/Hymn/Reflection

A Benedicite for creation

Let the chuckling brooks bless you, great God,
the quiet tarns sing your praise.
May the breaking waves and waterfalls bless you, Beloved,
praise your name and glorify you for ever.

Let the roaring forties bless you, great God,
the blue-green ocean sing your praise.
May the fjords and straits bless you, Beloved,
praise your name and glorify you for ever.

Let the mighty rivers bless you, great God,
the great lakes sing your praise.
May the placid canals bless you, Beloved,
praise your name and glorify you for ever.

THE SECOND SUNDAY BEFORE LENT

Let the limestone and chalk bless you, great God,
the sands and clays sing your praise.
May the slates and granites bless you, Beloved,
praise your name and glorify you for ever.

Let the cairns of the mountains bless you, great God,
the meadows and crops sing your praise.
May the marshes and forests bless you, Beloved,
praise your name and glorify you for ever.

Let the oaks and the elms bless you, great God,
the silver birches sing your praise.
May the chestnuts and beeches bless you, Beloved,
praise your name and glorify you for ever.

Let the albatrosses bless you, great God,
the penguins and dolphins sing your praise.
May the whales and the plankton bless you, Beloved,
praise your name and glorify you for ever.

Let the migrating swallows bless you, great God,
parrots and finches sing your praise.
May the soaring and weaving flocks bless you, Beloved,
praise your name and glorify you for ever.

Let the wolves of the tundra bless you, great God,
the dogs and the cats sing your praise.
May the gazelles and the snow leopards bless you, Beloved,
praise your name and glorify you for ever.

Let the world of the atom bless you, great God,
the genes and molecules sing your praise.
May the ceaseless dance of life bless you, Beloved,
praise your name and glorify you for ever.

THE SECOND SUNDAY BEFORE LENT

Let the breathing and pulsing planet bless you, great God,
this blue and white sphere sing your praise.
May the inhabitants of earth bless you, Beloved,
praise your name and glorify you for ever.

Let the sun and the moon bless you, great God,
the Milky Way sing your praise.
May the far-flung reaches of space bless you, Beloved,
praise your name and glorify you for ever.

Or:

The Beatitude of Simplicity

Blessed are the poor in spirit:
they are citizens of God's Domain.

Blighted are those who have everything,
blessed are those who have nothing.

We are weighed down by possessions,
our shoulders bowed down by craving and worry.
We spend too little time with our children,
we have forgotten the simplest of pleasures.
Bring us the blessing of restraint,
a willingness to do without what we thought we needed.
Humble us to be empty, to be nothing,
to be open to the simplest of gifts.
Remove from us our pride in our power,
give us trust in your wisdom and grace.
May the secret of living open up for us,
receiving the only wealth that endures.

Blighted are those who have everything,
blessed are those who have nothing.

THE SECOND SUNDAY BEFORE LENT

Gospel Acclamation

Alleluia, alleluia, alleluia.
Alleluia, alleluia, alleluia.

A   Have no anxious thought about tomorrow.
B   Not one thing came into being without the Word.
C   Jesus said to his disciples, Where is your faith?

Alleluia, alleluia, alleluia.

A reading from the Gospel according to Matthew/John/Luke
Alleluia, alleluia, alleluia.

A   *Matthew 6.25–34*
B   *John 1.1–14*
C   *Luke 8.22–25*

Give glory to the living God.
Alleluia, alleluia, alleluia.
Unfold the Living Word for us today.

Collects

Year A

Loving Presence,
   calming the anxieties of our hearts,
give us the grace to be as the birds of the air
   and the flowers of the field,
knowing that all creation is dependent
   on your sustaining power.
We pray this in the Spirit of the One
   who trusted you day by day,
   and who had nowhere to lay his head.

Year B

Living Communion,
   Harmony of Love, glorious Trinity,
complete and whole, yet creating without pause,
draw us into the spiral of your abundant life,
after the pattern of the One
   who embodied for us
      that unconditional and transforming love,
and enable us in the Spirit
   to play our singular part
      in the unfolding of the universe.

Year C

Living Presence of creative power,
   terrifying in intensity,
   in the chaos of the storm
      and the tumult of human desires,
help us to understand the power of the atom
   and the fury of our hearts,
that the energies of the universe
   and the passions of our bodies
      may be harnessed to serve the purposes of love,
in the Spirit of Jesus,
   powerful in word and deed.

4

Living Presence of light and truth,
   gently bringing us face to face
      with our weakness and fear,
give us courage
   to greet the stranger and the outcast with love,
      no longer banishing them from city or home,
      no longer freezing them from our hearts.
We pray this after the pattern of Jesus
   and in the power of the Spirit.

5

Living Presence of truth,
   leading us into what is deeply true,
   of which, as yet, we are unaware,
open our minds and lips,
   give us the words to speak the truth,
   words that take shape deep within us,
   words that do not distort or betray.
We pray this in the name of the One
   who lived the truth
   and is the way and the life.

6

Living Presence to the destitute,
   prune our lives of all that we cling to,
Living Presence to the wealthy,
   draw us through the narrow gate of loss,
Living Presence in Jesus,
   living in those whom we neglect,
through their generosity and forgiveness
   empower us to turn outwards
      from our self-centredness,
   to open our withered arms,
   and to embrace one another,
      reconciled at last.
We pray this after the pattern of the One
   who never ceases to forgive,
   seventy times seven and beyond.

The Sunday next before Lent

Kyries

We have betrayed our humanity by thinking of others or ourselves as destined for dust rather than for glory.

We have not brought the light of transfiguration into dark places.

We have not listened to the wisdom of the divinely human One, transfigured on the mountain.

Response/Canticle/Hymn/Reflection

The Transfiguration

Estranged from the light and the glory,
we miss the many-splendoured presence.
We see through veils and mists,
we glimpse through glass but darkly.
Like the people of old we dare not look on the faces
of those who have dared the presence of God.

Yet with unveiled faces we may believe
we shall behold the transfigured one,
the human being in whose destiny we share,
the light of the divine shining through us all.

The God who said, Let light shine in the darkness,
has shone in our hearts, has illuminated our minds,

THE SUNDAY NEXT BEFORE LENT

to give the light of the knowledge of the divine glory
in the face of Jesus transfigured on the mountain.

Our disfigured faces know affliction now,
yet we are being prepared for a weight of glory,
as we look not to the things that are seen,
but to those that are as yet unseen,
not to that which shall change and decay,
disintegrating into dust in the wind,
but to that which is eternal,
solid joys and lasting pleasure.

Or:

The Beatitude of Sorrow

Blessed are those who mourn:
they will find consolation.

Blighted are those who wallow in self-pity.
Blessed are those who grow through their sorrow.

We are thrown to the ground by grief,
the days are as bleak as the endless nights.
You have taken my companion away from me,
our years together suddenly cut short.
Why is life so unfair?
Why this trudge across this dreary wilderness?
We are tempted to sink into despair,
we harbour a bitterness that is eating us away.
Bring us the blessing of tears,
the gift of balm to hearts in anguish.
Give us the courage that endures through the dark,
the compassion that draw us closer to others.
We belong together in the fellowship of suffering,
which alone brings us to the borders of joy.

Blighted are those who wallow in self-pity.
Blessed are those who grow through their sorrow.

THE SUNDAY NEXT BEFORE LENT

Gospel Acclamation

Alleluia, alleluia, alleluia.
Alleluia, alleluia, alleluia.

A Jesus was transfigured before them and his face shone like the sun.
B This is my son, the beloved. Listen to him.
C With unveiled faces let us see the glory of the Christ.

Alleluia, alleluia, alleluia.

A reading from the Gospel according to Matthew/Mark/Luke

Alleluia, alleluia, alleluia.

A *Matthew 17.1–9*
B *Mark 9.2–9*
C *Luke 9.28–36 [37–43]*

Give glory to the living God.
Alleluia, alleluia, alleluia.
Unfold the Living Word for us today.

Collects

Year A

Living Presence of light and glory,
   illuminating the face of Jesus on the mountain,
give us courage steadily to look at him,
   as to a lamp shining in the dark,
until your day dawns in the murkiest places of our being,
and the morning star rises with radiance in our hearts.
We pray this in the Spirit of the One
   who is the Light of the world.

THE SUNDAY NEXT BEFORE LENT

Year B

Living Presence of dazzling darkness,
   of sight beyond our own sight,
   whose light in the face of Jesus
     struck his followers with awe,
   so that they did not know what they were saying,
reassure us in the midst of our fears
   that we too are your daughters and your sons
   in whom you take great delight.
We pray this in the Spirit of the One
   who is the Light of the world.

Year C

Living Presence of transfiguring light,
   revealing your power in the body of Jesus,
illuminate our dark and disfigured faces,
   shine forth from within the very cells of our being,
that we may be transformed from glory to glory,
   and so fulfil our destiny to be as one with you.
We pray this in the Spirit of the One
   who was transfigured on the mountain,
     Jesus, the Light of the world.

Collects for the rest of this week follow, under the heading Ash Wednesday.

Ash Wednesday
Years A, B, C

Kyries

We have not let our balloons of self-inflation be punctured.

We have not slimmed down enough to be able to slip through the needle's eye.

We have needled one another with needless wounds.

Gospel Acclamation

Alleluia, alleluia, alleluia.
Alleluia, alleluia, alleluia.

Where your treasure is, there also will be your heart.

Or:

Neither do I condemn you. Go, and sin no more.

Alleluia, alleluia, alleluia.

A reading from the Gospel according to Matthew/John

Alleluia, alleluia, alleluia.

ASH WEDNESDAY

Matthew 6.1–6, 16–21
Or:
John 8.2–11

Give glory to the living God.
Alleluia, alleluia, alleluia.
Unfold the Living Word for us today.

Collect

(See below for Collects for the weekdays after Ash Wednesday.)

Compassionate and loving Presence,
   forgiving us to seventy times seven,
   spreading gratitude in our hearts,
   releasing us from the guilt and power
     of all that paralyses us and drags us down,
inspire us to give generously,
   to fast thoughtfully,
   and to pray thankfully,
keeping this Lent in the Spirit of the One
   who bore the cost of love,
   enduring to the end.

For Penitence and Ashes

One: Recognition

A Litany of Penitence

Creator, Giver of Life,
pour mercy upon us.
Redeemer, Bearer of Pain,
pour mercy upon us.
Sanctifier, Maker of Love,
pour mercy upon us.

From all evil and wickedness,
from pride, vanity, and hypocrisy,
from rage, hatred, and malice,
and from all violent intent ...

Pause

God of freedom,
deliver us.

From a refusal to recognize our worth,
from persistence in self-hatred,
from collusion with powers that oppress us ...

Pause

God of freedom,
deliver us.

From sloth, envy, and greed,
from hardness of heart and contempt for the poor,
from rejection of those who disturb us ...

Pause

God of freedom,
deliver us.

From grasping lust and its delusions,
from the spirit of domination,
from deceit and falsehood and the subtleties of lying ...

Pause

God of freedom,
deliver us.

In all times of our sorrow,
in the tears of compunction,
in the piercing of our hearts with the lance of your love ...

ASH WEDNESDAY

Pause

God of freedom,
deliver us.

In all times of our failures,
in the nights of our pain,
in the hour of our dying ...

Pause

God of freedom,
deliver us.

From belief that you condemn,
in the judgement that discerns,
in the release of the truth ...

Pause

God of freedom,
deliver us.

Give us and those who oppress us true repentance,
forgive our negligence,
remove our blindness,
render us helpless to harm,
recall us to the way of wisdom.

Holy God,
refining us, merciful towards us,
holy and utterly loving,
pour mercy upon us.

Or:

Ten Invitations

1. Be loyal to the will of the One who draws you by a still, small voice.
   Prepare to listen by clearing your life of noise and clutter.
   Ask yourself what is your deepest desire ...

   Pause

   We have not been loyal.
   We have not responded to the call of true life.

2. Do not give ultimate loyalty to anything but the mysterious divine Creator-Lover.
   Live simply and generously wherever greed and addiction rule ...

   Pause

   We have not lived simply.
   We have been trapped in circles of compulsion.

3. Pay close attention simply to what is.
   Ask the questions that arise from such contemplation, and seek to respond in truth ...

   Pause

   We have not been aware.
   We have not dared to look and listen.

4. Be thankful for small deeds of kindness as well as for greater blessings,
   and allow the spirit of gratitude to melt the ice of fear and pain.
   Take time out of time – to rest and to be, to celebrate and to laugh ...

   Pause

   We have not been thankful.
   We have resisted the blessings that are offered.

ASH WEDNESDAY

5   Live steadfastly into the commitments you have made.
Face illusion and betrayal with truth and courage.
Delve ever deeper the mines of trust, forgiveness,
   and compassion ...

Pause

We have not dared.
We have become sour and embittered.

6   Welcome both neighbour and stranger as human beings to
   be accepted and valued
in the same way as you would wish to be received ...

Pause

We have not been generous.
We have been held in the grip of fear.

7   Make your contribution to the common good of your own
   country, and of the one world,
   of which you are a citizen.
Reverence the earth and replenish what you have taken ...

Pause

We have not been responsible.
We have retreated into private comforts.

8   Open your heart to kindness and compassion, towards
   others and towards yourself.
Respond to the lonely with care and tact.
Cast out fear by the presence and gentle persistence of
   prayerful and thoughtful affection.
Share the pain of those whose stories reveal harm and shame,
   and be with them without intrusion or possession.

Pause

We have not been sensitive.
We have hated the reminders of our own pain.

9 Refuse to act on feelings of superiority.
  Shun slogans.
  Bear the discomfort of what is unresolved.
  Listen silently to those who are different from yourself,
     without anxiety or hurry,
  and so avoid the strident claims of the fanatics and the
     self-righteous.
  Remember that each of us is contained within a whole that
     is greater than the sum of the parts ...

Pause

We have not been patient.
We have held ourselves aloof.

10 Be expectant of the future, in faith and hope,
   trusting that it will bring gifts beyond anything you could
      predict or imagine ...

Pause

We have resisted change.
We have become frozen by our past.

Two: Turning

Let us turn in heart and mind, in will and expectancy, to the
   Presence who is Love ...
Let us recognize love in every human being, above all in Jesus,
revealing in flesh and blood, in word and deed, the heart of the
   divine ...
Let our attention, our questions, our living, all be focused on
   the God
whose love is utterly truthful, shimmeringly joyous,
   transforming pain and enhancing life,
consistent and persistent, embracing all that would cause harm,
never letting go, pressing gently and for as long as need be into
   all that refuses to respond,

never ultimately excluding, banishing, or destroying that which
   is still being shaped,
created, repaired, restored, transformed.

Three: Release

In the Spirit of Christ we are released from all that traps us,
from our fear of love and our refusal to believe in our own
   worth,
from our desire for revenge against those who have hurt us,
from our need to live a lie, locked away from others,
from the ghetto to which we have banished our childlike selves,
from gnawing anxiety and the fear of death,
from a brooding sense of guilt and failure.
Let us in the Spirit of Christ claim our freedom,
let us be assured that we are accepted as we are and not for
   what we have achieved,
let us celebrate all that lifts us up in hope,
let us absorb the truth that we are enfolded in the love and
   peace of God.
Amen. Thanks be to God.

Holy loving God,
   in whom we live and move and have our being,
making us for yourself
   so that our hearts are restless till they rest in you,
refine us and strengthen our wills,
that no self-centred desires or weaknesses
   may hinder us from following you.

May we dwell upon your wisdom,
   folly to worldly cleverness.
In your light may we see light,
and in your service and friendship
   may we find our perfect freedom.
We pray this in the power of the Holy Spirit
   and in the name of Jesus Christ. **Amen.**

ASH WEDNESDAY

Four: From dust to dust

As a token this day of our penitence and of our deliverance
let us receive on our foreheads in ash the sign of the cross.
For we are dust and to dust we shall return.
Yet the sign of death has become for us the sign of hope,
and of life rising from the grave.

God of yearning, against whom we cannot ultimately resist,
mark us with your fierce love
and take us through our dying,
turn us outwards from self-centredness,
melt our anxieties and guilt and fear,
sweep away the ashes of the fires of our hatreds,
that we may face you,
our heart's desire and the whole world's joy.

Words accompanying the sign of the cross in ash:

Remember you are mortal.
You are dust and to dust you shall return.

Eternal God of love,
you unlock our prison doors,
you bring your healing touch,
you put behind you all our sin,
you show us that dust is not the end,
you confirm and strengthen us in goodness,
and you keep us in life eternal,
in and through Jesus Christ
whose bore the cost of love
and endured to the end.
Amen.

So let us journey with confidence into Lent.

ASH WEDNESDAY

God of the desert,
as we follow Christ into the unknown,
may we resist the temptations that will come our way.
May it be your bread that we eat,
your world that we serve,
and you alone whom we worship.
So be it. Amen.

Collects for the weekdays after Ash Wednesday

Thursday

Living Presence, yearning, inviting,
   whom we cannot for ever resist,
mark us with your fierce love
   and take us through our dying,
burn the fires of our hatreds
   to become as ash blown away in the wind,
gently prise us open
   from our shrunken turned-in selves,
that we may face you in tranquillity,
   and know you as our hearts' desire
      and the whole world's joy.
We pray this in the power of the Spirit
   and in the name of Jesus Christ.

Friday

Eternal Presence of love,
   unlocking our prison doors,
   touching us with pain-absorbing hands,
   dissolving the weight of evil that presses down upon us,
   revealing that dust is not the end,
surge through us with the energy of your Spirit,

ASH WEDNESDAY

that we may grow and mature
   in the ways of your freedom and healing,
     and in the paths of your goodness and your justice,
in and through Jesus Christ,
   who bore the cost of love,
     enduring to the end.

Saturday

Holy, loving Presence,
   pruning us of self-centred desires,
   strengthening us in our weaknesses,
so refine us in your Spirit
   that nothing may hinder us from following you,
after the pattern and in the name of Jesus Christ.

The First Sunday of Lent

Kyries

We have listened to the tempting voice and we have repeated our habitual follies.

We have been presented with times of testing and we have run to safety.

We have been faced by inevitable trials and we have shut our eyes in denial.

Response/Canticle/Hymn/Reflection

The Beatitude of Insecurity

Blessed are the gentle:
they will inherit the earth.

Blighted are those who are obsessed with security.
Blessed are those with nowhere to lay their heads.

Fear stalks the streets and we tremble,
we change the locks and strengthen the doors.
We build our walls thicker and higher,
the screech of our alarms pierces the night.
Yet still deep within we feel insecure,
we anxiously crave approval from others.

THE FIRST SUNDAY OF LENT

Away from home we are ill at ease,
nowhere do we feel we belong.
Bring us the blessing of the wanderers,
those content to be unrecognized, unknown.
Claiming nothing for ourselves,
we shall be given the freedom of the earth.
Nowhere now can we be in exile,
everywhere is simply our home.

Blighted are those who are obsessed with security.
Blessed are those with nowhere to lay their heads.

Gospel Acclamation

Alleluia, alleluia, alleluia.
Alleluia, alleluia, alleluia.

A   Let the Word of God dwell deep in your heart.
B   Do not resist the Spirit, who impels you into the wilderness.
C   Lay aside your idols and serve the living God.

Alleluia, alleluia, alleluia.

A reading from the Gospel according to Matthew/Mark/Luke
Alleluia, alleluia, alleluia.

A   *Matthew 4.1–11*
B   *Mark 1.9–15*
C   *Luke 4.1–13*

Give glory to the living God.
Alleluia, alleluia, alleluia.
Unfold the Living Word for us today.

THE FIRST SUNDAY OF LENT

Collects

Year A

Living Presence, fiercely loving,
   testing us to see if we ring true,
burn away our dross
   and refine us in the fire
      that alone can make us whole.
We pray this in the Spirit of the One
   who bore the cost of love,
      enduring to the end.

Year B

Living Presence, wise and holy,
   judging us gently
   yet loving us implacably,
lure us into the desert,
   drive us, if need be, into the wilderness,
where the air of truth is clear,
   the night of struggle sharp,
and where your gifts, to our surprise,
   meet our deepest need.
We pray this in the Spirit of the One
   who bore the cost of love,
      enduring to the end.

Year C

Living Presence of searing truth,
give us a steady will to refuse the temptation
   to exercise power by money, might, or magic,
and give us the grace and courage
   to live simply, gently, and honestly.
We pray this in the Spirit of the One
   who bore the cost of love,
      enduring to the end.

THE FIRST SUNDAY OF LENT

4

Living Presence of steadying strength,
   whose way is shown to us in Jesus,
      striving with temptation in the desert,
keep our eyes fixed on you,
   as trust and doubt,
   truth and falsehood,
   faithfulness and betrayal
      wax and wane through the years,
and give us courage to face the tests and trials
   that have yet to come our way.
We pray this after the pattern of Jesus
   and in the power of the Spirit.

5

Living Presence, wise and discerning,
   compassionate and just,
pierce our hearts
   that we may yield our secrets,
shake our faultlines
   that our pride may crumble to dust,
and cast your light upon our hidden murk,
   that, purified and strengthened in forgiveness and faith,
we may bear witness to your fierce and gentle rule.
We pray this is the power of the Spirit
   and in the name of Jesus Christ.

THE FIRST SUNDAY OF LENT

6
Living Presence,
   revealing the strength of love
      by being born a powerless child
      and dying a nail-torn outcast,
turn our eyes and desires
   from the seductions and trappings
      of worldly wealth and power,
and give us the courage to risk being vulnerable,
that we may take to ourselves
   all that will make us wise and truly human.
We pray this in the power of the Spirit
   and in the name of Jesus Christ.

The Second Sunday of Lent

Kyries

We have listened to the tempting voice and we have repeated our habitual follies.

We have been presented with times of testing and we have run to safety.

We have been faced by inevitable trials and we have shut our eyes in denial.

Response/Canticle/Hymn/Reflection

The Beatitude of Struggle

Blessed are those who yearn for justice to prevail:
they will be satisfied.

Blighted are those who are never disturbed.
Blessed are those who strive for righteousness.

We slump into complacency:
in our apathy nothing matters.
We are weary of struggling through storms,
we close our doors against the wind.
We have ceased to care:
we are too much at ease.

THE SECOND SUNDAY OF LENT

We are disintegrating,
already the dust we soon shall be.
Bring us the blessing of renewed desire,
an appetite for justice, a zest for life itself.
Make us hungry again for your way,
thirsty that your will be accomplished.
Only so shall we know deep content,
only so shall we at last become whole.

Blighted are those who are never disturbed.
Blessed are those who strive for righteousness.

Gospel Acclamation

Alleluia, alleluia, alleluia.
Alleluia, alleluia, alleluia.

A Listen to the wind, Nicodemus, listen to the wind.
B If you lose your life you will find it.
C How I desire to gather you together as a hen gathers her brood.

Alleluia, alleluia, alleluia.

A reading from the Gospel according to John/Mark/Luke
Alleluia, alleluia, alleluia.

A *John 3.1–17*
B *Mark 8.31–38*
C *Luke 13.31–35*

Give glory to the living God.
Alleluia, alleluia, alleluia.
Unfold the Living Word for us today.

THE SECOND SUNDAY OF LENT

Collects

Year A

Living Presence of the faiths,
  calling humanity to walk in trust,
calm our fears,
  quell our thirst for certainty,
  and show us the wisdom of insecurity,
always expectant of your gifts
  in the least expected places.
We pray this in the Spirit of the One
  who bore the cost of love,
  enduring to the end.

Year B

Living Presence, challenging, subversive,
  whose pressure our surface selves resist,
teach us
  not to hold on
    but to let go,
  not to protect ourselves
    but to be vulnerable,
  not to seek comfort and security
    but to give up what seems most dear,
so that our deeper selves may emerge
  and direct our lives.
We pray this in the Spirit of the One
  who bore the cost of love,
  enduring to the end.

THE SECOND SUNDAY OF LENT

Year C

Living Presence, unflinching in courage,
strengthen us to stand firm like the prophets of old,
   and speak the truth to those in power
     who do not wish to hear it.
We pray this in the Spirit of the One
   who bore the cost of love,
     enduring to the end.

4

Living Presence, always seeking to right what is wrong,
   whose will is our peace,
     founded not on military victory
     but on justice for all,
wean us from our inherited desire
   to survive at the expense of others,
   to separate ourselves from them,
   to feel superior and secure,
expand our hearts to include all others,
   receiving them into our lives
     as our equals before you,
   finding our security in ever-deepening trust,
   and so fulfilling through us
     your purposes for humankind.
So may we follow the Way of the Crucified One,
   participating in your costly giving love.

THE SECOND SUNDAY OF LENT

5

Mysterious Presence,
    choosing the small, the unnoticed, the obscure,
    to renew the ways of your covenant
    when your followers wander and fail you,
strive with our intractable clay,
    and enable us to love as Jesus did,
        emptied of power,
        untouched by delusion,
        dying unrecognized,
    yet for those with eyes opened by your Spirit
        the decisive clue to the mystery of your being.

6

Intimate Presence,
    flesh of our flesh,
    earth of our earth,
reveal to us the anger and malice,
    the greed and pride,
    that mask our pain;
give us strength to withdraw the spear of our revenge
    from the flesh of others,
    and from your flesh;
enclose our hurt in your side that we have wounded,
    and draw us closer to one another
        in compassion and forgiveness,
    dependent utterly on your mercy and acceptance.
We pray this after the pattern of Jesus
    and in the power of the Spirit.

The Third Sunday of Lent

Kyries

We have listened to the tempting voice and we have repeated our habitual follies.

We have been presented with times of testing and we have run to safety.

We have been faced by inevitable trials and we have shut our eyes in denial.

Response/Canticle/Hymn/Reflection

The Beatitude of Compassion

Blessed are the merciful:
mercy will be shown to them.

Blighted are those who show no compassion.
Blessed are those who forgive those who hurt them.

We become self-centred in our pain,
our grumbling the ground bass of our thoughts.
We are insensitive to the cries of others,
we shut our ears and refuse to hear.
We complain that no one understands us,
we wander a wasteland far distant from love.

THE THIRD SUNDAY OF LENT

Bring us the warmth we have forgotten we need,
surround our hurts with mercy's embrace.
Let us enter the domain of acceptance, of forgiveness,
our deepest joy to seventy times seven.

Blighted are those who show no compassion.
Blessed are those who forgive those who hurt them.

Gospel Acclamation

Alleluia, alleluia, alleluia.
Alleluia, alleluia, alleluia.

A The living water that I give will spring up in you to eternal life.
B Become a living temple, yourself a house of prayer.
C Let the tree of your life be pruned that you may bear much fruit.

Alleluia, alleluia, alleluia.

A reading from the Gospel according to John/Luke
Alleluia, alleluia, alleluia.

A *John 4.5–42*
B *John 2.13–22*
C *Luke 13.1–9*

Give glory to the living God.
Alleluia, alleluia, alleluia.
Unfold the Living Word for us today.

THE THIRD SUNDAY OF LENT

Collects

Year A

Living Presence,
   flowing through human lives
      like water springing up in desert places,
quench our thirst,
   we who have become dry and shrivelled,
invigorate us,
   that we may stride forth once more on our journey,
and gladden our hearts
   that we may walk with a spring in our step.
We pray this in the Spirit of the One
   who bore the cost of love,
      enduring to the end.

Year B

Living Presence,
   constant and true,
   angry at our corruptions of heart and deed,
refine us and purify us,
   that we may become,
      as buildings and as bodies,
         houses of prayer,
            temples where all are welcome,
            shrines where your name is honoured.
We pray this in the Spirit of the One
   who bore the cost of love,
      enduring to the end.

THE THIRD SUNDAY OF LENT

Year C

Living Presence, fiercely loving,
    working in us and among us to our greatest good,
give us courage to face without flinching
    temptation, test, and trial,
trusting that you will give us
    the strength to win through.
We pray this in the Spirit of the One
    who bore the cost of love,
        enduring to the end.

4

Living Presence, all-embracing,
    Creator of each and everyone,
loving us equally and completely,
    constant in compassion,
    patient in repair,
    softening hardened hearts,
may your grace and power heal the bodies
    of all who wander far from love's domain,
and reconcile and restore
    all that is torn and gone awry.
We pray this in the Spirit of the One
    who forgave those who knew not what they did.

THE THIRD SUNDAY OF LENT

5

Loving Presence, tender and compassionate,
   revealing your nature to us
      when you are most vulnerable,
      defenceless and naked,
clear from our lives
   all that keeps us defended from the truth,
   the clutter of possessions and clothes,
      words and fears,
that we may recognize one another
   as sisters and brothers in your love.
We pray this after the pattern of Jesus
   and in the power of the Spirit.

6

Living Presence, repairing and restoring,
   your heart moving with compassion
      to enfold those who cry out in their distress,
come as healing water in our desert place,
   give comfort to those who are grieving,
   and courage to those who are weakening,
that even in the midst of suffering and dying,
   despair may be banished and hope revived.
We pray this in the Spirit of the Crucified One,
   the bearer of our pain.

The Fourth Sunday of Lent – Mothering Sunday

Kyries

We have sometimes been too angry with one another.

We have sometimes ignored one another.

We have not always helped one another with the chores.

Response/Canticle/Hymn/Reflection

The Beatitude of Truth
Blessed are the pure in heart:
they will see God.

Blighted are those who live in delusion.
Blessed are those set free by the truth.

We float away in a bubble of fantasy,
distracted, detached from our truest selves.
We wander in a land of delusions,
haunted by fears with no substance.
We reach out for the baubles that glitter,
that crumble to dust in our hands.

THE FOURTH SUNDAY OF LENT – MOTHERING SUNDAY

Bring us the chastening wind of your truth,
chasing our ghosts into oblivion.
Refine us in the crucible that tests us,
distilling the silver from all that is impure.
With the most sobering of truths that we ignore
give us entrance to a life that is free.

Blighted are those who live in delusion.
Blessed are those set free by the truth.

Gospel Acclamation

Alleluia, alleluia, alleluia.
Alleluia, alleluia, alleluia.

A One thing I know: once I was blind, now I can see.
B Receive the gift of eternal life.
C Your brother was dead and has come to life; he was lost and has been found.

Alleluia, alleluia, alleluia.

A reading from the Gospel according to John/Luke
Alleluia, alleluia, alleluia.

A *John 9.1–41*
B *John 3.14–21*
C *Luke 15.1–3, 11b–32*

Give glory to the living God.
Alleluia, alleluia, alleluia.
Unfold the Living Word for us today.

THE FOURTH SUNDAY OF LENT – MOTHERING SUNDAY

Collects

Year A

Living Presence,
　giving yourself in utter love
　　to ease all fear from our hearts,
warm us out of our suspicion of strangers
　into the generous welcome
　　that heralds the making of friends.
We pray this in the Spirit of the Universal Christ,
　the Resurrection and the Life.

Year B

Living Presence of abundant love and life,
　with compassion and steady voice
　　calling us by name,
quieten the beat of condemnation
　that we drum into our ears
　　and into the ears of others,
and reassure us that we belong to one another
　in the fold of your heart.
We pray this in the Spirit of the Universal Christ,
　the Resurrection and the Life.

Year C

Source of our life,
　calling us by the sound of running water,
　we who are parched by drought,
refresh us at the wellspring
　to which the shepherd guides us,
even the Universal Christ,
　the Resurrection and the Life.

THE FOURTH SUNDAY OF LENT – MOTHERING SUNDAY

4

Wise and loving Shepherd,
   guiding your people in the ways of your truth,
   leading us through the waters of baptism,
   and nourishing us with the food of eternal life,
keep us in your mercy,
   and so guide us through the perils of evil and death,
   that we may know your joy
      at the heart of all things,
   both now and for ever.
We pray this in the Spirit of the Universal Christ,
   the Resurrection and the Life.

5

Shining Presence,
   revealing to us a vision of beauty,
   shaped from the least likely matter of your creation,
sustain us in desperate days,
   even in the midst of desolation,
that, graced and cheered,
   we may not perish
   but be encouraged to glory.
We pray this in the Spirit of the Universal Christ,
   the Resurrection and the Life.

6

Living Presence,
   whose power is persistent and patient
      and never threatening,
disarm the mighty of this world
   and calm their fears,

THE FOURTH SUNDAY OF LENT – MOTHERING SUNDAY

gently remove the cataracts from their eyes,
    that they may weep tears of compunction,
        and see their enemies as human beings,
    and come to know them as the only friends
        who bear the gift of their salvation,
in Yeshua, powerless yet victorious in love for us.

The Fifth Sunday of Lent
(Passiontide begins)

Kyries

We have kept silent when we should have spoken.

We have spoken when we should have kept silent.

We have been guilty of denial and betrayal.

Response/Canticle/Hymn/Reflection

The Beatitude of Reconciliation

Blessed are the peacemakers: they will be called the daughters and the sons of God.

Blighted are those who are at war with themselves.
Blessed are those who embrace the cost of reconciliation.

Discord harries us, deep in our hearts,
emerging to spread division and hatred.
The seeds of a plant top heavy with pride
breed our downfall and ruin.
We dominate by muscle and voice,
the doormats seethe with resentment.

THE FIFTH SUNDAY OF LENT

Bring us face to face, however wary we be,
till our eyes melt into tentative trust.
Fill us with the spirit of goodwill,
till we recognize the other as human.
Give us courage to dissolve evil with goodness,
that damage may be repaired and relationships restored,
that we may indeed become friends,
alive in the righteousness that leads to true peace.

Blighted are those who are at war with themselves.
Blessed are those who embrace the cost of reconciliation.

Gospel Acclamation

Alleluia, alleluia, alleluia.
Alleluia, alleluia, alleluia.

A In the darkness of your tombs, hear the summons, Lazarus, Come forth.
B When a grain of wheat dies into the earth, it bears much fruit.
C Hear the call of God in the dying and rising of Jesus.

Alleluia, alleluia, alleluia.

A reading from the Gospel according to John
Alleluia, alleluia, alleluia.

A *John 11.1–45*
B *John 12.20–33*
C *John 12.1–8*

Give glory to the living God.
Alleluia, alleluia, alleluia.
Unfold the Living Word for us today.

THE FIFTH SUNDAY OF LENT

Collects

Year A

Living Presence of abundant life,
   whose light penetrates the darkness of the tomb,
summon us,
   trapped in death-dealing ways,
   bound by our own or others' folly,
and release us into the freedom for which we yearn.
We pray this in the Spirit of the One
   who bore the cost of love,
   enduring to the end.

Year B

Living Presence,
   suffering with us,
   taking to your heart
      the evil, pain, and death of your world,
   revealing your nature once and for all
      in Jesus of the Cross,
give us courage to face whatever comes our way,
   that all that drags us down
      may become the means
         whereby we are transformed to glory.
We pray this in the Spirit of the One
   who bore the cost of love,
   enduring to the end.

Year C

Mysterious Presence,
    present at the heart of the world's dying and rising,
    revealing to us the deepest truths in Jesus,
give us courage to trust
    that evil will be dissolved in goodness,
    that pain will be transfigured to joy,
    and that death will be swallowed up by life;
and may we know this new life
    in the encounters of our everyday lives
    and in the cells deep within our being.
We pray this in the Spirit of the One
    who bore the cost of love,
    enduring to the end.

4

Silent Presence,
    from whom so often we receive no answers,
    yet to whom we pray lest we despair,
justify your ways to us,
    and do not silence us, like Job,
        with power and grandeur,
that we may be convinced again
    of the invincible strength
        of vulnerable and crucified love,
    even when Golgotha and genocide
        seem worlds apart.
We pray this in the Spirit of the One
    whose cry echoed through the daytime's darkness
        of the hill outside the city.

5

Living Presence of love –
 if indeed you are love,
 for our howls of suffering have hidden your face –
show us again in the Crucified One
 the eyes telling us that you are there,
 at the heart of the desolate cries.
We pray this in the Spirit of Jesus,
 who loved his own even to the end,
 and kept on trusting
  even when there was no answer to his cry.

6

Silent Presence,
 holding to yourself the awesome cry
 that would shatter us if we heard it,
take to yourself the cries of our battered hearts,
 the cries of those burdened by constant pain,
 the cries of those bowed down by oppression,
 the sounds that we bring
  so that we may not be silent.
Hear us in the name of Jesus,
 whose forsaken cry
 from the pinioned cross
 pierced the earth and sky.

Palm Sunday
Years A, B, C

Kyries

We have kept silent when we should have spoken.

We have spoken when we should have kept silent.

We have been guilty of denial and betrayal.

Response/Canticle/Hymn/Reflection

The Beatitude of Life

Blessed are the persecuted for the cause of justice:
theirs is the Freedom of the City of God.

Blighted are those who die by degrees.
Blessed are those who know life abundant.

We shrivel in the wind of our winters,
fear stares out of hearts that are frozen.
Cold eyes stab with hatred,
a persecuting spirit sharpens the steel.
Those who stand up for justice and truth
reveal us as shallow, full of petty contempt.

PALM SUNDAY

Bring us the spirit of steadfastness,
that we may not flinch at insult and slander.
Fill us with the spirit of endurance,
when our purses are taken, our legs shackled.
Enable us to face death with cheerfulness,
for only so will we live to the full.

Blighted are those who die by degrees.
Blessed are those who know life abundant.

And/Or:

He slowly rides, in poverty,
towards his dark extremity,
ignores the war horse at the gate,
a donkey's back his chosen fate.

The horse of Pilate's pomp and might,
the soldiers armed, prepared to fight,
display the reach of empire's hand
from Rome to furthest eastern land.

The donkey of his gentle power –
persistent, faithful, hour by hour –
so weak and foolish to their eyes,
can stun the world with God's surprise.

Death's vultures soon will gather round,
unjust and cruel voices sound,
but stones shall shake, love's power shall surge,
new unexpected life emerge.

What is the path your feet have trod?
What is your hope? Who is your God?
Resplendent with bejewelled crowns?
Or Fool of fools and Clown of clowns?

Gospel Acclamation

For the Palm Gospel

Alleluia, alleluia, alleluia.
Alleluia, alleluia, alleluia.

A Your king comes to you riding on a donkey.
B Blessed is the one who comes in the name of our God.
C If you are silent even the stones will cry out.

Alleluia, alleluia, alleluia.

A reading from the Gospel according to Matthew/Mark/Luke
Alleluia, alleluia, alleluia.

A Matthew 21.1–11
B Mark 11.1–11
C Luke 19.28–40

Give glory to the living God.
Alleluia, alleluia, alleluia.
Unfold the Living Word for us today.

For the Gospel of the Passion

Alleluia, alleluia, alleluia.
Alleluia, alleluia, alleluia.

A Truly this man was a son of God.
B Jesus made no further response, so that Pilate was amazed.
C Truly I tell you, today you will be with me in paradise.

Alleluia, alleluia, alleluia.

A reading from the Gospel according to Matthew/Mark/Luke
Alleluia, alleluia, alleluia.

A *Matthew 26.14–27.66 or 27.11–54*
B *Mark 14.1–15.47 or 15.1–39 [40–47]*
C *Luke 22.14–23.56 or 23.1–49*

Give glory to the living God.
Alleluia, alleluia, alleluia.
Unfold the Living Word for us today.

Collect

Living Presence of justice,
　　showing us in Jesus
　　　　that all who proclaim and embody your way
　　　　　　will suffer at the hands of the powers that be,
give us courage to enact that way in our lives,
　　whatever the consequences,
and encourage us with moments
　　when relationships are made right again,
so filling us with hope that in you all shall be well.
We pray this in the Spirit of the One
　　who indeed bore the cost of love,
　　　　enduring to the end,
　　and is alive in us and in you for ever.

Monday of Holy Week
Years A, B, C

Kyries

We have kept silent when we should have spoken.

We have spoken when we should have kept silent.

We have been guilty of denial and betrayal.

Response/Canticle/Hymn/Reflection

Father, forgive these soldiers who crucify me:
they know not what they do.
**The divine love sees far with compassion,
with justice tempered by mercy,
not knowing how not to forgive.**

Today you shall be with me in Paradise:
for you have met your moment of truth.
**The divine love embraces those who are humbled,
who have faced their fear and admitted their need.**

Friend, so much loved, see, your mother:
mother, so much loved, see, your son.
**The divine love is enfleshed in human loving,
as we receive each other as gifts.**

MONDAY OF HOLY WEEK

Facing the terror of abandonment he cried:
My God, my God, why have your forsaken me?
**The divine love is all but overwhelmed,
obscured by the power of pain.**

Stricken, parched, in agony he cried,
I thirst, I thirst.
**The divine love groans through the worst,
never letting go, never giving up.**

My task is completed,
it is finished, fulfilled, it is done.
**The divine love has kept faith,
shining with light at the very moment of death.**

He commended his whole being to God,
to the One from whom he came.
**The divine love draws us close:
we can trust that all shall be well.**

Gospel Acclamation

Alleluia, alleluia, alleluia.
Alleluia, alleluia, alleluia.

Give from your hearts and do not count the cost.
Alleluia, alleluia, alleluia.

A reading from the Gospel according to John
Alleluia, alleluia, alleluia.

John 12.1–11

Give glory to the living God.
Alleluia, alleluia, alleluia.
Unfold the Living Word for us today.

MONDAY OF HOLY WEEK

Collect

Living Presence,
 revealing to us our true humanity in Jesus,
evoke in our hearts and deeds a generosity
 that gives beyond the bounds of common sense
 and offends the crabby and the mean.
We pray this in the Spirit of the One
 who indeed bore the cost of love,
 enduring to the end,
 and is alive in us and in you for ever.

Tuesday of Holy Week
Years A, B, C

Kyries

We have kept silent when we should have spoken.

We have spoken when we should have kept silent.

We have been guilty of denial and betrayal.

Response/Canticle/Hymn/Reflection

Father, forgive these soldiers who crucify me:
they know not what they do.
**The divine love sees far with compassion,
with justice tempered by mercy,
not knowing how not to forgive.**

Today you shall be with me in Paradise:
for you have met your moment of truth.
**The divine love embraces those who are humbled,
who have faced their fear and admitted their need.**

Friend, so much loved, see, your mother:
mother, so much loved, see, your son.
**The divine love is enfleshed in human loving,
as we receive each other as gifts.**

TUESDAY OF HOLY WEEK

Facing the terror of abandonment he cried:
My God, my God, why have your forsaken me?
The divine love is all but overwhelmed,
obscured by the power of pain.

Stricken, parched, in agony he cried,
I thirst, I thirst.
The divine love groans through the worst,
never letting go, never giving up.

My task is completed,
it is finished, fulfilled, it is done.
The divine love has kept faith,
shining with light at the very moment of death.

He commended his whole being to God,
to the One from whom he came.
The divine love draws us close:
we can trust that all shall be well.

Gospel Acclamation

Alleluia, alleluia, alleluia.
Alleluia, alleluia, alleluia.

The grain that dies into the earth bears much fruit.
Alleluia, alleluia, alleluia.

A reading from the Gospel according to John
Alleluia, alleluia, alleluia.

John 12.20–36

Give glory to the living God.
Alleluia, alleluia, alleluia.
Unfold the Living Word for us today.

TUESDAY OF HOLY WEEK

Collect

Mysterious Presence,
   bringing to human beings
      moments of truth and destiny,
keep us alive to such times of testing
   that we may recognize the hour when it comes,
   and not be afraid.
We pray this in the Spirit of the One
   who indeed bore the cost of love,
      enduring to the end.

Wednesday of Holy Week
Years A, B, C

Kyries

We have kept silent when we should have spoken.

We have spoken when we should have kept silent.

We have been guilty of denial and betrayal.

Response/Canticle/Hymn/Reflection

Father, forgive these soldiers who crucify me:
they know not what they do.
**The divine love sees far with compassion,
with justice tempered by mercy,
not knowing how not to forgive.**

Today you shall be with me in Paradise:
for you have met your moment of truth.
**The divine love embraces those who are humbled,
who have faced their fear and admitted their need.**

Friend, so much loved, see, your mother:
mother, so much loved, see, your son.
**The divine love is enfleshed in human loving,
as we receive each other as gifts.**

Facing the terror of abandonment he cried:
My God, my God, why have your forsaken me?
The divine love is all but overwhelmed,
obscured by the power of pain.

Stricken, parched, in agony he cried,
I thirst, I thirst.
The divine love groans through the worst,
never letting go, never giving up.

My task is completed,
it is finished, fulfilled, it is done.
The divine love has kept faith,
shining with light at the very moment of death.

He commended his whole being to God,
to the One from whom he came.
The divine love draws us close:
we can trust that all shall be well.

Gospel Acclamation

Alleluia, alleluia, alleluia.
Alleluia, alleluia, alleluia.

The time has come for the glory of the truly Human One to be revealed.
Alleluia, alleluia, alleluia.

A reading from the Gospel according to John
Alleluia, alleluia, alleluia.

John 13.21–32

Give glory to the living God.
Alleluia, alleluia, alleluia.
Unfold the Living Word for us today.

Collect

Piercing Presence,
 revealing to us the secrets of our hearts,
 and bearing the pain of our betrayals,
be with us when we realize
 that the night has engulfed us,
do not let us sink into despair,
and keep alive in us the Spirit of the One
 who indeed bore the cost of love,
 enduring to the end.

Maundy Thursday
Years A, B, C

Kyries

We have neglected the means of grace, your Presence with us now in this sacrament.

We have not kept vigil with those in distress.

We have been guilty of betrayals, we have deserted and fled through fear.

Response/Canticle/Hymn/Reflection

Father, forgive these soldiers who crucify me:
they know not what they do.
The divine love sees far with compassion,
with justice tempered by mercy,
not knowing how not to forgive.

Today you shall be with me in Paradise:
for you have met your moment of truth.
The divine love embraces those who are humbled,
who have faced their fear and admitted their need.

Friend, so much loved, see, your mother:
mother, so much loved, see, your son.
The divine love is enfleshed in human loving,
as we receive each other as gifts.

Facing the terror of abandonment he cried:
My God, my God, why have your forsaken me?
The divine love is all but overwhelmed,
obscured by the power of pain.

Stricken, parched, in agony he cried,
I thirst, I thirst.
The divine love groans through the worst,
never letting go, never giving up.

My task is completed,
it is finished, fulfilled, it is done.
The divine love has kept faith,
shining with light at the very moment of death.

He commended his whole being to God,
to the One from whom he came.
The divine love draws us close:
we can trust that all shall be well.

Gospel Acclamation

Alleluia, alleluia, alleluia.
Alleluia, alleluia, alleluia.

In washing your feet, do you know what I have done to you?
Alleluia, alleluia, alleluia.

A reading from the Gospel according to John
Alleluia, alleluia, alleluia.

John 13.1–17, 31b–35

Give glory to the living God.
Alleluia, alleluia, alleluia.
Unfold the Living Word for us today.

MAUNDY THURSDAY

Collects

1

Disturbing Presence,
   turning our lives inside out,
   showing us in Jesus
      that to be a nameless nobody
         is the way to the truth of ourselves and of you,
give us the grace and courage to recognize
   that it is at the point of nothing
   that we are embraced by you
   and welcomed freely into your domain.
We pray this in the Spirit of the One
   who indeed bore the cost of love,
      enduring to the end.

2

Living Presence,
   inspiring Jesus to share with us
      through bread and wine
         the deepest meaning of your love,
open our eyes
   that we may see you present and alive to us
      in the breaking and remembering of the bodybread
         and the pouring of the life-giving bloodredwine.
We pray this in the Spirit of the One
   who indeed bore the cost of love,
      enduring to the end.

Good Friday
Years A, B, C

Kyries

We have drawn back from paying the cost of love and justice.

We have not given of ourselves utterly.

We have not trusted the way of the cross to be the way of life.

Response/Canticle/Hymn/Reflection

Father, forgive these soldiers who crucify me:
they know not what they do.
**The divine love sees far with compassion,
with justice tempered by mercy,
not knowing how not to forgive.**

Today you shall be with me in Paradise:
for you have met your moment of truth.
**The divine love embraces those who are humbled,
who have faced their fear and admitted their need.**

Friend, so much loved, see, your mother:
mother, so much loved, see, your son.
**The divine love is enfleshed in human loving,
as we receive each other as gifts.**

GOOD FRIDAY

Facing the terror of abandonment he cried:
My God, my God, why have your forsaken me?
The divine love is all but overwhelmed,
obscured by the power of pain.

Stricken, parched, in agony he cried,
I thirst, I thirst.
The divine love groans through the worst,
never letting go, never giving up.

My task is completed,
it is finished, fulfilled, it is done.
The divine love has kept faith,
shining with light at the very moment of death.

He commended his whole being to God,
to the One from whom he came.
The divine love draws us close:
we can trust that all shall be well.

Gospel Acclamation

Alleluia, alleluia, alleluia.
Alleluia, alleluia, alleluia.

The work has been done. It is finished.
Alleluia, alleluia, alleluia.

A reading from the Gospel according to John
Alleluia, alleluia, alleluia.

John 18.1 – 19.42

Give glory to the living God.
Alleluia, alleluia, alleluia.
Unfold the Living Word for us today.

GOOD FRIDAY

Collect

Living Presence of mysterious power
    and unfathomable love,
  revealing to us in Jesus
  that it is through the perplexing places
    of evil, pain, and death,
  that the whole of anguished humankind
    and the groaning universe itself
  will come to the place of joy and wonder,
give us courage steadfastly to trust
  that in the end we shall come to know
  that all has been done well.
We pray this in the Spirit of the One
  who indeed bore the cost of love,
    enduring to the end.

An act of remembrance of the participants in the Passion

[At each name, at the end of the first line, a bell may be tolled.]

It was at the ninth hour, at three in the afternoon, that Jesus died.

At such an hour a passing bell might toll.

John Donne wrote:
'Who bends not his ear to any bell,
which upon any occasion rings?
But who can remove it from that bell
which is passing a piece of himself out of this world?
No man is an island, entire of itself:
every man is a piece of the main;
if a clod be washed away by the sea,
Europe is the less, as well as if a promontory were,
as well as if a manor of thy friends or of thine own were;
any man's death diminishes me,

GOOD FRIDAY

because I am involved in mankind;
and therefore never send to know for whom the bell tolls:
it tolls for thee.'

Let us bring to mind those whose stories have been woven into the drama of the Passion of Jesus, along with countless human beings before and since who have played similar parts in the unfolding of this world's story:

Simon the leper,
who was hospitable to Jesus at Bethany ...
and all those who have been rejected,
and yet sheltered the persecuted and outcast ...

The unnamed woman,
who anointed Jesus with expensive ointment ...
and all who have given of themselves with reckless generosity ...

Judas Iscariot, who betrayed Jesus ...
and all who have sold their friends out of fear or greed or from mistaken loyalties ...

Peter the Rock,
who denied Jesus but whose heart was true ...
and all who have let others down through cowardice, yet have repented and been forgiven ...

The disciple whom Jesus loved,
who lay close to him at the Last Supper ...
and all who have found through their love for each other something of the love of God ...

The young man who followed Jesus to Gethsemane ...
and all who have been attracted to Jesus and his Way ...

The disciples who slept in the garden and then ran away ...
and all who have fled through weakness from a test of courage ...

GOOD FRIDAY

Caiaphas the high priest,
who acted out of loyalty to his tradition ...
and all who have refused the deeper challenges of their ancestors' faith ...

Herod, bewitched by a desire for dazzling displays of magic ...
and all who have yearned for knowledge and power alone,
without the way of faithand love at heart ...

Pilate the governor,
colluding with Caiaphas to dispose of a troublemaker ...
and all those who have enforced the law at the expense of justice ...

The soldiers,
who did their job, but with cruelty ...
and all who have misused the law with excess of force ...

Simon of Cyrene,
who was compelled to carry the cross ...
and all who have been forced to obey an oppressor's whim ...

The thief who repented and the thief who did not ...
and all who have been faced with their past life at their last hour on earth ...

The bystanders and the crowd,
who mocked and bayed and gaped ...
and all those who have been swept along by rhetoric to do harm ...

The centurion,
who was impressed by the way Jesus died ...
and all who have been moved to a moment of faith by the example of others ...

GOOD FRIDAY

Mary Magdalene, Mary the mother of James and Joses,
Salome, and the other women,
who had ministered to Jesus, and now looked on at a distance ...
and all who have been forced to serve within the limits set
them by those in power ...

Mary the mother of Jesus,
whose heart was pierced, but who bore him there still ...
and all who have been sore wounded by the unjust death of
those they loved ...

Joseph of Arimathea,
who was bold to ask Pilate for the corpse of Jesus ...
and all who have found within themselves unexpected reserves
of courage ...

Nicodemus,
who had come to Jesus at night ...
and all who have listened to the wind and done good, even if
by stealth ...

At the ninth hour Jesus cried out with a loud voice,
'Eloi, Eloi, lama sabachthani?',
which means, 'My God, my God, why have you forsaken me?'
And some of the bystanders hearing it said, 'He is calling
Elijah.'
And one ran, and filled a sponge full of vinegar and put it on a
reed and gave it to him to drink.
'Wait, let us see whether Elijah will come to take him down.'
And Jesus uttered a loud cry, and breathed his last.

Easter Eve
Years A, B, C

Kyries

We find it hard to wait when all is dark.

We have stayed by the graveside and refused to live in new ways.

We have been entombed and refused your summons to 'come out' into the day.

Gospel Acclamation

Alleluia, alleluia, alleluia.
Alleluia, alleluia, alleluia.

Do not lose hope, even in the most desolate places.
Alleluia, alleluia, alleluia.

A reading from the Gospel according to John
Alleluia, alleluia, alleluia.

John 19.38–42

Give glory to the living God.
Alleluia, alleluia, alleluia.
Unfold the Living Word for us today.

Collect

Thou ... Mystery ... Hidden ...
   so often silent ...
   seeming not to hear our cries of grief and desolation,
renew in us the spirit of hope,
   and even in the deepest darkness
   may we hear the approach of the One
     who harrows hell,
   and greets even Judas with a kiss.

Easter Day

Kyries

The power of the risen Christ sets us free from evil's grip!

The touch of the risen Christ heals our deepest wounds and sorrow!

The life of the risen Christ swallows up our fear of death!

Response/Canticle/Hymn/Reflection

Christ is risen. Alleluia!
Christ is risen. Alleluia!
Let the gospel trumpets sound far and wide,
penetrating and clear in the light of dawn.
Atgyfododd Crist. Alelwia!
Atgyfododd Crist. Alelwia!
Let servers and satellites send out the good news,
in an instant encircling the globe.
Christus ist auferstanden. Alleluia!
Christus ist auferstanden. Alleluia!
With the torch that heralds the games
let each runner hand on the good news.
Le Christ est resuscité. Alleluia!
Le Christ est resuscité. Alleluia!
Let the flames spread inextinguishable,
encircling the earth with a ring of fire.

Christos aneste. Alleluia!
Christos aneste. Alleluia!
Let all creation stretch into life with jubilant shout:
our travail is ended, death's grip is released.
Christos voskrese. Alleluia!
Christos voskrese. Alleluia!
Let the still small voice whisper in the garden,
Let the Sun light up our faces with glory.
Christ is risen. Alleluia!
Christ is risen. Alleluia!

Gospel Acclamation

Alleluia, alleluia, alleluia.
Alleluia, alleluia, alleluia.

- A Christ is alive in you, risen from the dead.
- B Christ is risen! Do not be afraid.
- C Do not look for the living among the dead. Christ is risen.

Alleluia, alleluia, alleluia.

A reading from the Gospel according to John/Matthew/
Mark/Luke
Alleluia, alleluia, alleluia.

- A *John 20.1–18 or Matthew 28.1–10*
- B *John 20.1–18 or Mark 16.1–8*
- C *John 20.1–18 or Luke 24.1–12*

Give glory to the living God.
Alleluia, alleluia, alleluia.
Unfold the Living Word for us today.

Collects

Year A

Mysterious Presence,
   revealing to us our true humanity in Jesus,
   planting the truth in each and every one of us
     by his resurrection,
empower us on this day to rise from the dead,
   that we may know that he is alive in us for ever.
We pray this in the Spirit of the Universal Christ,
   the Resurrection and the Life.

Year B

Enlivening Presence,
   penetrating the sleeping cells of our bodies,
call us again to wake up,
   to rise from the dead,
that the life may shine forth from within us.
We pray this in the Spirit of the Universal Christ,
   the Resurrection and the Life.

Year C

Living Presence,
   gracious and graceful,
   in Jesus drawing alongside
     our distraught and grieving selves,
   gently whispering to us by name,
bring us to the joy that knows
   that your voice will never be stilled,
and to the calm where all despair melts away.
We pray this in the Spirit of the Universal Christ,
   the Resurrection and the Life.

4

Living Presence,
   raising us from our death-dealing,
   giving us life in abundance,
work in us the power and wisdom of your love,
   and make it visible among us as your justice.
We pray this in the Spirit of the Universal Christ,
   the Resurrection and the Life.

5

Living Presence of merciful tenderness,
   giver of life and swallower of death,
gently embrace our weakness and pain,
   and bring us to health and wholeness,
that we may sing a new song of joy and delight.
We pray this in the Spirit of Yeshua,
   redeeming the powers,
   giving hope to humankind,
   calling us to follow this perplexing path to glory.

6

Living Presence of light and life,
   breaking the bonds of death,
shine on us with eyes of compassion,
   let light flood the dungeons
     of our rejected and downtrodden selves,
so that the oppressed may go free,
   the weak rise up in strength,
   and the hungry be fed,
     now, in these our days.
We pray this in the Spirit of the pioneer
     of our liberation,
   our elder brother, and our faithful friend.

The Second Sunday of Easter

Kyries

The power of the risen Christ sets us free from evil's grip!

The touch of the risen Christ heals our deepest wounds and sorrow!

The life of the risen Christ swallows up our fear of death!

Response/Canticle/Hymn/Reflection

Christ is risen. Alleluia!
Christ is risen. Alleluia!
Death and life have engaged each other in a wondrous struggle,
and death is swallowed up by life.
Christ is risen. Alleluia!
Life is renewed, more solid and more real,
shot through with colours deep and radiant.
Christ is risen. Alleluia!
Glory shines through everything that is,
illuminating our scars and deepest wounds.
Christ is risen. Alleluia!
Love most costly has prevailed:
unconquerable is its power.
Christ is risen. Alleluia!
Sleeping cells, awake from the dead:
the light will shine out from within you.

THE SECOND SUNDAY OF EASTER

Christ is risen. Alleluia!
Embrace the living hope!
Death has no final word!
Christ is risen. Alleluia!
In the resurrection of Jesus
is life in God for ever.
Christ is risen. Alleluia!

Gospel Acclamation

Alleluia, alleluia, alleluia.
Alleluia, alleluia, alleluia.

A Blessed are those who have not seen, and yet believe.
B If you forgive the sins of any they are forgiven.
C Jesus came and stood among them and said, Peace be with you.

Alleluia, alleluia, alleluia.

A reading from the Gospel according to John
Alleluia, alleluia, alleluia.

John 20.19–31

Give glory to the living God.
Alleluia, alleluia, alleluia.
Unfold the Living Word for us today.

THE SECOND SUNDAY OF EASTER

Collects

Year A

Living Presence of eternal life,
   playing an enduring melody deep within our hearts,
empower us to hear and transmit the chords
     that never die,
   the music of justice and compassion,
   the melodies of forgiveness and peace.
We pray this in the Spirit of the Universal Christ,
   the Resurrection and the Life.

Year B

Living Presence of abundant life,
   your voice resonating deep within our being,
raise us from depression, despair, and death,
   that we may be filled with the energy
     of gratitude and joy.
We pray this in the Spirit of the Universal Christ,
   the Resurrection and the Life.

Year C

Living Presence,
   overflowing with love,
   drawing us to one another,
     that we might recognize our common humanity
     and bring the gifts that each of us uniquely bears,
hold before us the vision
   of the universal Human One,
     the Christ whose roots are deep within your being,
   and who is alive in us,
     the pioneer of the way of love for humankind.
We pray this in the Spirit of the Universal Christ,
   the Resurrection and the Life.

4

Living Presence,
   holding us to the embrace
     of the One who lures us by love,
keep our eyes fixed on the goal of our journey,
   that we may never lose sight of your justice
   and step by step may be fleet of foot and heart.
We pray this in the Spirit of the pioneer
    of our salvation,
   our elder brother, and our faithful friend.

5

Living Presence in the dark hours,
challenging us to cherish their silence
   and not be afraid,
may we find that the silence
   is not empty but full of presence,
may we find at its heart
   not a storm but the love that calms our fears,
may we know the gentle touch of a trustworthy hand
   stretched out to us in the night.
We pray this in the Spirit of Jesus,
   our pattern and our guide.

6

Pain-bearing Presence,
   moving with our wounds to heal them,
   bringing joy in the midst of suffering,
sound the note of your presence in our afflictions,
   and create such music with us
     as the world has not yet heard.
We pray this in the Spirit of the Universal Christ,
   the Resurrection and the Life.

The Third Sunday of Easter

Kyries

The power of the risen Christ sets us free from evil's grip!

The touch of the risen Christ heals our deepest wounds and sorrow!

The life of the risen Christ swallows up our fear of death!

Response/Canticle/Hymn/Reflection

This is a day of rejoicing,
given for our joy and delight.
Our hearts warm with gladness,
we feast with laughter and song.

The stone which the builder rejected
has become the head of the corner.
Those we despised and dismissed
have become beautiful in our sight.
Those we have injured and harmed
have brought salve and healing to our wounds.
Those we drew back from in fear
have found courage to embrace us with gentleness.
The strangers we encircled with unease
have found ways to teach us their wisdom.
Our own inner child we have banished
has called us to come out and play.

THE THIRD SUNDAY OF EASTER

If the hairs of our heads are numbered,
how can we doubt that we matter to God?
As the people of old shouted for joy,
let children yet unborn hear its sound.
For even the darkness dazzles with light,
and love floods our bodies with radiance.

This is a day of rejoicing,
given for our joy and delight.
Our hearts warm with gladness,
we feast with laughter and song.

Gospel Acclamation

Alleluia, alleluia, alleluia.
Alleluia, alleluia, alleluia.

A Jesus was known to them in the breaking of the bread.
B Jesus stood among them and said, Peace be with you.
C Jesus said, How much do you love me?

Alleluia, alleluia, alleluia.
A reading from the Gospel according to Luke/John
Alleluia, alleluia, alleluia.

A *Luke 24.13–35*
B *Luke 24.36b–48*
C *John 21.1–19*

Give glory to the living God.
Alleluia, alleluia, alleluia.
Unfold the Living Word for us today.

Collects

Year A

Living Presence, companion on our journey,
    drawing close to us in strangers on the road,
open our minds and hearts
    to the living word brought by those
        we do not know,
    and to the nourishing food
        offered by scarred hands.
We pray this in the Spirit of the Universal Christ,
    the Resurrection and the Life.

Year B

Mysterious and hidden Presence,
    giving us glimpses of what we should like to know,
strengthen our faltering trust
    in your gift of life being sufficient for us,
that there will be light enough for our path,
    and that all will be glorified
        in the presence of the Universal Christ,
        the Resurrection and the Life.

Year C

Living Presence of searing truth,
    questioning us with eyes that see through us,
    yet renewing us in your love this day
        through bread and wine,
give us grace to receive the love
    that is being offered to us by those around us,
by the presence in them of the Universal Christ,
    the Resurrection and the Life.

4

Living Presence, indomitable, steadfast,
  going ahead of us as a mountain guide,
encourage us to climb the rugged path,
  strengthen us to face the perils of storm and hunter,
  and show us again that your steadfast love
    is stronger than anything else in the universe.
We pray this in the Spirit of Jesus,
  the pioneer of the new and living way.

5

Living Presence,
  restorer of the years that we have lost,
  that the locusts have eaten,
give to us the future
  that we thought we should never see,
make of the present moment
  a firstfruit of true liberation,
and even when we feel exiled,
  locked in, despairing,
move secretly within us and among us,
  and without our realizing it,
    keep us moving on our journey to your city.
We pray this in the Spirit of the Universal Christ,
  the Resurrection and the Life.

6

Living Presence in the dark despairing depths,
  hearing the cry from our throats
    parched with drought,
  and the gasp of terror in the abyss
    opened up by our folly,
hold us firm in our struggle with you,
  fierce, fiery lover,

THE THIRD SUNDAY OF EASTER

do not let us escape
 from our unseen yet greatest good,
and so let some new glory be wrought,
 and new and unexpected life come to birth.
We pray this in the Spirit of the Universal Christ,
 the Resurrection and the Life.

The Fourth Sunday of Easter

Kyries

The power of the risen Christ sets us free from evil's grip!

The touch of the risen Christ heals our deepest wounds and sorrow!

The life of the risen Christ swallows up our fear of death!

Response/Canticle/Hymn/Reflection

We praise you, O Christ,
risen from the dead,
breaking death's dominion,
rising from the grave.

Absorbing in yourself
the force of evil's ways,
you destroyed death's age-old sting
and are alive for evermore.

Let us find our life in you,
breaking through our fear of everlasting void.
For you are risen from the dead,
the firstfruits of those who sleep.

THE FOURTH SUNDAY OF EASTER

From the days of first awareness
we betrayed the call of life,
**yet yearned for that communion
which still we dimly sense.**

Pain and evil, malice and cruel greed,
these deepened the sorrow of our hearts.
**Yet they are done away in light of glorious dawn,
the victory of resurrection day.**

At one with all who've lived,
so all of us have died;
**at one with your humanity
all shall be made alive.**

Gospel Acclamation

Alleluia, alleluia, alleluia.
Alleluia, alleluia, alleluia.

A Let us hear your voice, Good Shepherd, calling us by name.
B Let us know you, Good Shepherd, as you know us.
C Call us, Good Shepherd, and bid us follow you.

Alleluia, alleluia, alleluia.

A reading from the Gospel according to John
Alleluia, alleluia, alleluia.

A *John 10.1–10*
B *John 10.11–18*
C *John 10.22–30*

Give glory to the living God.
Alleluia, alleluia, alleluia.
Unfold the Living Word for us today.

Collects

Year A

Living Presence,
  giving yourself in utter love
    to ease all fear from our hearts,
warm us out of our suspicion of strangers
  into the generous welcome
    that heralds the making of friends.
We pray this in the Spirit of the Universal Christ,
  the Resurrection and the Life.

Year B

Living Presence of abundant love and life,
  with compassion and steady voice
    calling us by name,
quieten the beat of condemnation
  that we drum into our ears
    and into the ears of others,
and reassure us that we belong to one another
  in the fold of your heart.
We pray this in the Spirit of the Universal Christ,
  the Resurrection and the Life.

Year C

Source of our life,
  calling us by the sound of running water,
  we who are parched by drought,
refresh us at the wellspring
  to which the shepherd guides us,
even the Universal Christ,
  the Resurrection and the Life.

4

Wise and loving Shepherd,
    guiding your people in the ways of your truth,
    leading us through the waters of baptism,
    and nourishing us with the food of eternal life,
keep us in your mercy,
    and so guide us through the perils of evil and death,
    that we may know your joy
        at the heart of all things,
    both now and for ever.
We pray this in the Spirit of the Universal Christ,
    the Resurrection and the Life.

5

Shining Presence,
    revealing to us a vision of beauty,
    shaped from the least likely matter of your creation,
sustain us even in desperate days,
    and in the midst of desolation,
that, graced and cheered,
    we may not perish
    but be encouraged to glory.
We pray this in the Spirit of the Universal Christ,
    the Resurrection and the Life.

6

Living Presence,
   whose power is persistent and patient
      and never threatening,
disarm the mighty of this world
   and calm their fears,
gently remove the cataracts from their eyes,
   that they may weep tears of compunction,
      and see their enemies as human beings,
      and come to know them as the only friends
         who bear the gift of their salvation,
      in Yeshua, powerless yet victorious in love for us.

The Fifth Sunday of Easter

Kyries

The power of the risen Christ sets us free from evil's grip!

The touch of the risen Christ heals our deepest wounds and sorrow!

The life of the risen Christ swallows up our fear of death!

Response/Canticle/Hymn/Reflection

The dawn has crept upon us,
dispelling the shadows of night.
Into our darkness and sorrows,
in the valley of pain, of evil, of death,
the light spills over the mountain ridge,
the warmth stirs us to life renewed.
The Sun of Righteousness rises in our hearts,
empowering us to enact the signs of justice.
The vision of the risen Christ lifts us out of gloom,
the mark of the wounds now shining with light,
transfiguring even our shrivelled flesh,
awakening our sleeping cells to come to our aid.
For the tomb-bursting cry has shattered the night,
and your name resounds through the universe.

THE FIFTH SUNDAY OF EASTER

Gospel Acclamation

Alleluia, alleluia, alleluia.
Alleluia, alleluia, alleluia.

A   Simply believe, and you will do great things for God.
B   Abide in the vine, and so bear much fruit.
C   Let your love for one another be God's word among you.

Alleluia, alleluia, alleluia.

A reading from the Gospel according to John
Alleluia, alleluia, alleluia.

A   *John 14.1–14*
B   *John 15.1–8*
C   *John 13.31–35*

Give glory to the living God.
Alleluia, alleluia, alleluia.
Unfold the Living Word for us today.

Collects

Year A

Living Presence of the future,
  moving cloud, pillar of fire,
revealing yourself to us in Jesus,
  the pioneer of the living way,
go before us on our journey,
  give us courage to die our little deaths,
  and bring to life in us
    your unexpected gifts of grace.
We pray this in the Spirit of the Universal Christ,
  the Resurrection and the Life.

THE FIFTH SUNDAY OF EASTER

Year B

Constant Presence,
   loving through all its dyings
     the creation that is coming to be,
   inviting us to take our part
     in such a great endeavour,
test us with loving our brothers and sisters
   whom we meet day by day,
and with loving each small task that comes our way,
that we may show
   that we have not rejected your love,
   and have accepted the cost of creating.
We pray this in the Spirit of the Universal Christ,
   the Resurrection and the Life.

Year C

Living Presence of resilient and unfailing love,
   awesome in its challenges,
   gentle in its judgement,
empower us to bear the beams of love,
that we may reflect its penetrating light
   and embracing warmth,
     to enemies as well as to friends.
We pray this in the Spirit of the Universal Christ,
   the Resurrection and the Life.

4

Living Presence,
   the Way, the Truth, and the Life,
give us courage always to be loyal to the truth,
   and to follow wherever the way may lead,
     costly though it be,
trusting that the goal is none other than life with you.
We pray this after the pattern of Jesus
   and in the power of the Spirit.

5

Living Presence,
    taking to yourself the silent cries of those
        who are deeply depressed and in despair,
renew in us the spirit of hope,
    the yearning for life to surge through us once more,
    and the expectancy
        that even when every door is closed
            you will surprise us with joy.
We pray this after the pattern of Jesus
    and in the power of the Spirit.

6

Loving Presence of mysterious wrath,
    yet not destructive as we are in our rage,
pierce us with the heat and light that serve the truth,
    and in your fiercely compassionate anger
    overcome our murdering and mortality.
We pray this after the pattern of Jesus
    and in the power of the Spirit.

The Sixth Sunday of Easter

Kyries

The power of the risen Christ sets us free from evil's grip!

The touch of the risen Christ heals our deepest wounds and sorrow!

The life of the risen Christ swallows up our fear of death!

Response/Canticle/Hymn/Reflection

In your tender compassion and infinite wisdom,
even through the needle's eye of darkness and death,
you are drawing us into a marvellous light,
and giving us an abundance of life,
of freedom and room to breathe and dance again,
in the living Spirit of the risen Jesus.
Even now may the light of Christ
dawn on our flesh and blood,
illuminate our hearts and minds,
and draw us closer in the Presence.
Shine among us this day in your glory,
brighter than a thousand suns.

THE SIXTH SUNDAY OF EASTER

Gospel Acclamation

Alleluia, alleluia, alleluia.
Alleluia, alleluia, alleluia.

A   Abide in my love. Love one another. Keep my word.
B   Love one another as I have loved you.
C   Let not your hearts be troubled, neither let them be afraid.

Alleluia, alleluia, alleluia.

A reading from the Gospel according to John
Alleluia, alleluia, alleluia.

A   *John 14.15–21*
B   *John 15.9–17*
C   *John 14.23–29 or John 5.1–9*

Give glory to the living God.
Alleluia, alleluia, alleluia.
Unfold the Living Word for us today.

Collects

Year A

Living Presence of eternal life and unbounded love,
   in whose Spirit Jesus never stopped loving
   and swallowed even death itself,
deepen our awareness of your presence,
that we too may love and live, in you, for ever.
We pray this in the Spirit of the Universal Christ,
   the Resurrection and the Life.

THE SIXTH SUNDAY OF EASTER

Year B

Living Presence of friendship,
   calling us not to be slaves but to be friends,
inspire us and enable us to live up to our calling,
   each day giving at least a little
      for the good of our friends,
that one day we may be willing to give all
   for their well-being.
We pray this in the Spirit of the One
   who gave his life for his friends,
   and is alive in them for ever.

Year C

Living Presence of the peace
   that is more marvellous than we could understand,
   which again and again we fail to give to one another,
   and which we so desperately need,
renew in us the gift that you have promised,
   calm our troubled hearts,
   and melt our every fear,
that we may let your peace spread through us,
   so that, calm and centred,
      we may become peacemakers
         in our communities and throughout the world.
We pray this in the Spirit of the Universal Christ,
   the Resurrection and the Life.

Ascension Day
Years A, B, C

Kyries

The power of the risen Christ sets us free from evil's grip!

The touch of the risen Christ heals our deepest wounds and sorrow!

The life of the risen Christ swallows up our fear of death!

Response/Canticle/Hymn/Reflection

The One who walked as one of us,
in the Spirit obedient to the call,
in the sight of all created powers:
Ascended Christ, we greet you! Alleluia!

You have been proclaimed among the nations,
believed in throughout the world,
transfigured into glory:
Ascended Christ, we greet you! Alleluia!

We have set our hope on you,
the human face of God,
the Liberator of all the world:
Ascended Christ, we greet you! Alleluia!

Gospel Acclamation

Alleluia, alleluia, alleluia.
Alleluia, alleluia, alleluia.

He lifted up his hands and blessed them.
Alleluia, alleluia, alleluia.

A reading from the Gospel according to Luke
Alleluia, alleluia, alleluia.

Luke 24.44–53

Give glory to the living God.
Alleluia, alleluia, alleluia.
Unfold the Living Word for us today.

Collect

Welcoming and all-embracing Presence,
draw us to yourself,
   clay bound as we are,
transform us body and soul,
surge through our hearts and lift us up,
that we may follow the Pioneer of the Way
   into the cloud of your mysterious Presence,
and find ourselves most strangely at home.
We pray this in the Spirit of the Universal Christ,
   the Resurrection and the Life.

Friday and Saturday

Living Presence,
    becoming conscious in us as the universe evolves,
lift us up from all that would drag us down,
    and bring us and all creation to glory,
pioneered for us by the One
    who was and is fully conscious of matter
    transformed into a marvellous light,
risen, ascended, glorified.

Seventh Sunday of Easter

Kyries

The power of the risen Christ sets us free from evil's grip!

The touch of the risen Christ heals our deepest wounds and sorrow!

The life of the risen Christ swallows up our fear of death!

Response/Canticle/Hymn/Reflection

Te Deum (second part)

Universal Christ,
we greet you in your glory,
hidden deep in the being of God,
Word made flesh to deliver us,
brought to life by human touch,

glad to be born of Mary,
embodying the divine,
withdrawing the sting of death,
terrifying us with love unbounded,
offering to fulfil all we could desire,
opening the road to God's presence for ever,
guarding the freedom of the creation,
yearning for the gathering of the harvest.

Come, then, judge and deliver us,
who are freed at the cost of your life;
give us integrity to refuse what is evil,
give us your Spirit to discern what is true,
and lead us with all your saints
to lands of eternal glory.

Gospel Acclamation

Alleluia, alleluia, alleluia.
Alleluia, alleluia, alleluia.

Consecrate us in the truth, that we may be one,
that the world may believe and see your glory.
Alleluia, alleluia, alleluia.

A reading from the Gospel according to John
Alleluia, alleluia, alleluia.

A *John 17.1–11*
B *John 17.6–19*
C *John 17.20–26*

Give glory to the living God.
Alleluia, alleluia, alleluia.
Unfold the Living Word for us today.

Collects

Year A

Living Presence,
   entrusting to us such awe-inspiring power
   that we struggle to understand the nature of your gift,
   and tremble as we seek to use it aright,

set before us again the way of Yeshua,
    and work through us in your Spirit,
that we may steward that power in ways that do not bind
    others,
    but that free them to take their share with us
        in the inheritance of life and in the shaping of the future.
So may we grow tall, yet humble,
    in the Spirit of the Universal Christ,
    the Resurrection and the Life.

Year B

Living Presence,
    whose will it is that we should flourish,
    guiding us to oases in the desert of faithlessness,
nourish us again with the living water of your word,
that we may bring forth fruit that will last.
We pray this in the Spirit of the Universal Christ,
    the Resurrection and the Life.

Year C

Living Presence rejoicing,
    celebrating the Great Day of laughter and song,
whose Spirit wells up within us even now,
    ripples of joy flowing from our bellies,
    living water flowing through out deserts,
inspire all the true of heart
to delight in one another's love.
We pray this in the Spirit of the Universal Christ,
    the Resurrection and the Life.

4

Loving Presence,
   whose healing and forgiving power
      frees us from our paralysis
and binds us together as one,
so empower us in your Spirit
   that we may discover that we can do as Jesus did,
   even that greater things are possible for us.
We pray this in the Spirit of the universal Christ,
   incarnate and glorified,
      humanity alive in you for ever.

5

Living, loving Presence,
   taking to yourself the pains of the world,
cherish our wounded hearts in a tender embrace
   and cradle our scars,
that we may witness to the way of the pain-bearer,
   whose nailmarks shine in glory.
We pray this after the pattern of Jesus,
   in solidarity with one another,
      and in the power of the Spirit.

6

Holy Presence,
   teaching us not to be afraid of anything you have created,
   however threatened or repelled we may feel,
fill us with your Holy Spirit,
   that we may draw near to transform whatever we encounter.
We pray this in the same Spirit
   who finds a home in our flesh and blood.

Pentecost (Whit Sunday)
Years A, B, C

Kyries

For those times when our faith has seized up through fear,
and we have neglected the gifts of the Spirit:

For those times when our hope has slumped towards despair,
and we have neglected the gifts of the Spirit:

For those times when our love has been drained by apathy,
and we have neglected the gifts of the Spirit.

Response/Canticle/Hymn/Reflection

Creating Spirit, brooding over the formless deep,
breathing life into all that is coming to be,
we open our flesh that you may breathe through us.

From the depths of our being
we praise you for the surge of life.

Holy Spirit, cleansing and cool from the mountains,
breathing into us air that is sharp and astringent,
we wait for the gift of holiness that is yours alone.

From the depths of our brokenness
we praise you for the balm of healing.

PENTECOST

Life-giving Spirit, wind from every quarter of the earth,
breathing into our dry bones that they may live,
we lie as dead before you, silent as the grave.

From the depths of our decay
we praise you for the rise of new life.

Or:

O living flame that shines and warms
melt now the fear in every heart,
that we by eye and touch and word
may show that love's the finest art.

O kindly, fierce, refining fire
that gently strips our dross and rust,
disperse our smoke-self in the breeze,
and light our flame-self, true and just.

O running stream, now tumbling fast,
now flowing silently and deep,
renew us when we faint and fall,
and put our anxious thoughts to sleep.

Mysterious well, beyond our sight,
release the water long held fast,
which rises up to slake our thirst:
the ancient nectar ne'er surpassed.

O howling wind that shakes and tears,
that plucks the heart and skins the bone,
restrain your force, yet do your work,
and scour us clean, despite our groan.

O playful breeze that licks around
the walls and roof of home and church,
enliven us with questions deep,
with doubt and dance in onward search.

O earth and flesh, though seeming dust,
engage with water, wind, and flame,
take shape as human, Spirit charged,
who brings to life, and loves by name.

So earth and heaven shall be one,
as particle and wave conjoin,
a universe transformed by light,
for ever human and divine.

Gospel Acclamation

Alleluia, alleluia, alleluia.
Alleluia, alleluia, alleluia.

Listen to the words.
Listen to the wind.
Listen to the silence.
Alleluia, alleluia, alleluia.

A reading from the Gospel according to John
Alleluia, alleluia, alleluia.

A   John 20.19–23 or 7.37–39
B   John 15.26–27; 16.4b–15
C   John 14.8–17 [25–27]

Give glory to the living God.
Alleluia, alleluia, alleluia.
Unfold the Living Word for us today.

PENTECOST

Collects

Year A

Saving, healing, and liberating Presence,
   with us in the midst of our distress,
   forgiving our wrongdoing,
   relieving our suffering,
   loosening the chains that bind,
deepen our trust in your Spirit at work among us,
that your love may overwhelm us with joy
   and your hand lift us into the dance of freedom,
after the pattern of Jesus,
   alive in us for ever.

Year B

Living Presence,
   calling to us again and again in the power of your Spirit,
awaken us to your presence in our midst,
that our hearts may leap with the joy of our Alleluias,
   and with the trust of our Amens,
and so be given courage through all that is to come,
after the pattern of Jesus,
   alive in us for ever.

Year C

Living Presence, in each and all without distinction,
   yearning to bring us together in compassion and justice,
renew in us, and in all the nations of the world,
   the language that binds us as one,
written on every face and heard in every cry,
in the power of your Spirit,
   and after the pattern of Jesus,
   alive in us for ever.

Wednesday in the week following Pentecost

Living God,
   inspiring and illuminating our embodied selves
   with the gift of your Holy Spirit,
surge through us with such abundant love
   in our hearts and wills
that, with knowledge and understanding,
   and with wise discernment,
we may choose aright
   in all the hard decisions we have to make.
We pray this after the pattern of Jesus,
   alive in us for ever.

Thursday in the week following Pentecost

Living Presence
   melting the ice of our fears,
   stream through us
      in your Spirit of power and of love and of a sound mind,
after the pattern of Jesus, alive in us for ever.

Friday in the week following Pentecost

Living Presence,
   struggling with us for a more just world,
restrain us from those actions
   that tighten the mesh of the impoverished and oppressed,
keep us from pride in our strength and cleverness,
and keep us from despair when evil seems entrenched,
that your Spirit of freedom and wisdom and hope
   may bring us together to work for the common good,
after the pattern of Jesus,
   alive in us for ever.

Saturday in the week following Pentecost

Indwelling Presence,
 strengthen your servants with your heavenly grace,
that we may continue yours for ever,
 and daily increase in your Holy Spirit more and more,
 until our lives are shaped by the justice that marks your
  commonwealth
and we glimpse the glory of a world transformed
 in relationships made right.
We pray this after the pattern of Jesus
 and in the power of the Spirit.

Trinity Sunday

Kyries

Giver of life, we neglect your gift of life,
and we turn away from giving life to others.

Bearer of pain, we forget you share our suffering,
and we turn away from the anguish of others.

Maker of love, we refuse the cost and glory of love,
and we turn away from loving others.

Response/Canticle/Hymn/Reflection

Te Deum (first part)

Men and women:
praise the God of love!
Earth and sky:
worship the Creator!
Angelic powers of light eternal,
penetrating the ancient dark:
lift your voices with the song:
Holy, holy, holy, strange mysterious power,
the whole creation is full of your glory.

Saints and holy fools of every generation,
sing alleluia, alleluia.

Prophets crying out for justice,
sing alleluia, alleluia.
Martyrs who carried you in their wounds,
scars embodied in their glory,
sing alleluia, alleluia.
Your holy and stumbling people
in all times and places,
sing alleluia, alleluia.

Giver of life, of splendour and wonder,
tender, of infinite patience!
Bearer of pain, graceful and true,
with wounds bringing salve!
Maker of love, flaming and passionate,
guiding us into the truth!

Gospel Acclamation

Alleluia, alleluia, alleluia.
Alleluia, alleluia, alleluia.

A Glory to the Giver of Life.
    Glory to the Bearer of Pain.
    Glory to the Maker of Love.
B Listen to the wind, Nicodemus, listen to the wind.
C The Spirit of truth will guide you into all truth.

Alleluia, alleluia, alleluia.

A reading from the Gospel according to Matthew/John
Alleluia, alleluia, alleluia.

A *Matthew* 28.16–20
B *John* 3.1–17
C *John* 16.12–15

Give glory to the living God.
Alleluia, alleluia, alleluia.
Unfold the Living Word for us today.

Collects

Year A

Living Presence, beyond all names,
   overflowing with creative and redeeming energy,
   continually giving life, bearing pain, making love,
draw us ever closer in your mysterious Presence,
for in you is our destiny and delight,
   Lover, Beloved, and Mutual Friend.

Year B

Living Communion, Three-in-One, One-in-Three,
   distinguishable but not separable,
   source and goal of everything that is,
   that has been, and that is coming to be,
sweep us up into such life and love
   as we have yet but barely known,
making us partners in your work
   of creative and transforming power.

Year C

Mysterious One,
   beyond whose embrace nothing and no one can fall,
   showing us in Jesus that nothing that is truly human
     can ever be separated from what is truly divine,
encourage us into the fullness of humanity
   whose depths are indeed utterly divine,
a living communion of glory.

TRINITY SUNDAY

Wednesday after Trinity Sunday

Living Presence of divine communion,
   sharing your substance and your very self,
may we hear the gracious invitation to share
   the hospitality of your table and the dance of your love,
that together we may take delight in everything
   that you have created for our mutual joy.
We take our prayer and ourselves
   into the spiralling whirl and dance of the Trinity,
   Giver of life, Bearer of pain, Maker of love.

Thursday after Trinity Sunday – Corpus Christi

Living Presence,
   inspiring Jesus to share with us in bread and wine
   the deepest meaning of your love,
open the eyes of our bodies and our hearts
   that we may know you alive and present to us
   in the breaking and re-membering of the bodybread,
   and the pouring of the life-giving bloodredwine.
We pray this in the Spirit of the One
   who bore the cost of love, enduring to the end.

Friday after Trinity Sunday

Living Communion of harmony,
   complete and whole,
   making and mending without pause,
draw us into your abundant life,
   after the pattern of the One who embodied for us
     that creative and transforming love,
and so enable us in the Spirit
   to play our singular part in the unfolding of the universe,
and draw us closer into the mutual delight
   of the Three-in-One and One-in-Three.

Saturday after Trinity Sunday

All-embracing Presence, the Three-in-One,
   containing within your being acceptance and abandonment,
bring warmth and affirmation to our rejected and despairing
   selves,
awaken us to your presence
   in the word and the bread and the wine,
   in the touch and the water,
   in the wind and the fire,
that we may come alive and alight
   after the pattern of Jesus,
   in the power of the Spirit,
   and in the communion of your love.

The Sunday between 29 May and 4 June

(The Sunday between 24 and 28 May: use material for the Sunday between 17 and 23 February)

Kyries

We have lusted in our hearts and with our eyes.

We have not always kept our promises.

We have turned away from learning the more difficult lessons of love.

Response/Canticle/Hymn/Reflection

The First Commandment

I am the Lord your God:
you shall have no other gods but me.
You shall love the Lord your God with all your heart,
with all your soul, with all your mind,
and with all your strength.

Be loyal to the will of the Living One
who draws you by a still small voice.
Prepare to listen
by clearing your life of noise and clutter.

Ask yourself in the silence,
What is your deepest desire?

Silence

I am the Lord your God:
you shall have no other gods but me.
You shall love the Lord your God with all your heart,
with all your soul, with all your mind,
and with all your strength.

Gospel Acclamation

Alleluia, alleluia, alleluia.
Alleluia, alleluia, alleluia.

A   Be wise and not foolish: build your life on rock.
B   Let human need come before the letter of the law.
C   Trust in the word that heals.

Alleluia, alleluia, alleluia.

A reading from the Gospel according to Matthew/Mark/Luke
Alleluia, alleluia, alleluia.

A   *Matthew 7.21–29*
B   *Mark 2.23–3.6*
C   *Luke 7.1–10*

Give glory to the living God.
Alleluia, alleluia, alleluia.
Unfold the Living Word for us today.

THE SUNDAY BETWEEN 29 MAY AND 4 JUNE

Collects

Year A

Living Presence, wise and discerning,
  seeing deep into the human heart,
alert us to the truth that prayers merely spoken
  are worth nothing without the deeds of love,
that we may indeed find that we have built our lives on rock.
We pray this after the pattern of Jesus
  and in the power of the Spirit.

Year B

Living Presence, wise and discerning,
  whose wisdom guards the boundaries of our freedom,
enable us to distinguish between
  the regulations that oppress and
  the laws through which we mature and grow,
that we may become instruments
  of your just and compassionate rule.
We pray this after the pattern of Jesus
  and in the power of the Spirit.

Year C

Living Presence, healing, repairing,
  yearning to restore humankind –
  we who are so often divided and torn apart,
work through our care for one another,
  through the skills you call us to use,
  and through our trust in the gifts that you offer us,
that together we may become whole.
We pray this after the pattern of Jesus
  and in the power of the Spirit.

4

Living Presence, with truthful eye and loving heart,
give us grace so to look on those who oppose us
that we may seek to understand one another
   and discover together a better future
than either of us can discern alone.
We pray this in the Spirit of Jesus,
   whose eye challenged and encouraged and consoled.

5

Living Presence, wise and discerning,
   delivering us from the delusion
     that we are better than others,
give us clear and steadfast wills
   that we may refuse to condemn one another,
and give us knees that bend in humility
   before those we have wronged,
     knowing only their mercy and truth,
in the presence and after the pattern of Jesus,
   and in the power of the Spirit.

6

Living Presence, truthful and merciful,
   whose voice we miss amid the distractions of our lives,
penetrate the core of our being,
that we may hear and be glad,
   knowing ourselves accepted in your love,
able once again to live by your truth and your forgiveness.
We pray this after the pattern of Jesus
   and in the power of the Spirit.

The Sunday between 5 and 11 June

Kyries

We have not always controlled our anger.

We have sometimes been afraid of expressing our anger
when others have been unjust towards us.

We have not always channelled our anger
when we have become aware of injustice and have not acted.

Response/Canticle/Hymn/Reflection

The Second Commandment

You shall not make for yourself any idol.
God is spirit,
and those who worship God must worship in spirit and in truth.

Beware of giving loyalty to lesser gods,
worshipping celebrity, money, and power.
Trust only the Mystery,
the One who is beyond all names.
Where greed and addiction rule,
let us live without envy, simply and generously.

Silence

You shall not make for yourself any idol.
God is spirit,
and those who worship God must worship in spirit and in truth.

Gospel Acclamation

Alleluia, alleluia, alleluia.
Alleluia, alleluia, alleluia.

- A Hear of the merciful and healing God.
- B If you do the will of God you are Christ's sister, brother, mother.
- C Listen for the call that raises us to new life.

Alleluia, alleluia, alleluia.

A reading from the Gospel according to Matthew/Mark/Luke
Alleluia, alleluia, alleluia.

- A *Matthew 9.9–13,18–26*
- B *Mark 3.20–35*
- C *Luke 7.11–17*

Give glory to the living God.
Alleluia, alleluia, alleluia.
Unfold the Living Word for us today.

THE SUNDAY BETWEEN 5 AND 11 JUNE

Collects

Year A

Living Presence, compassionate, healing,
    gently quietening our guilt and our bargaining,
    ever pouring upon us your mercy
    and drenching us with your love,
open our hearts and minds and bodies,
    even to the deepest places of our being,
that we may gratefully receive your gifts,
    and delight in your presence with a light heart,
        a settled mind, a spring in our step,
        and the profound peace that surpasses our understanding.
We pray this after the pattern of Jesus
    and in the power of the Spirit.

Year B

All-embracing Presence,
    calling us out from lesser loyalties
        into a greater family and household,
give us courage to recognize our brothers and sisters
    in those we usually pass by,
and give us the trust to be vulnerable
    to those we think will reject us,
that we may show forth among us
    your commonwealth of justice and generosity.
We pray this after the pattern of Jesus
    and in the power of the Spirit.

Year C

Living Presence,
    whose love reaches beyond the boundary of death,
    whose word stirs us from our apathy,
    and whose touch gently melts our fears,

THE SUNDAY BETWEEN 5 AND 11 JUNE

ease us from the paralysis that grips us,
    that we may leap for joy and live again.
We pray this after the pattern of Jesus
    and in the power of the Spirit.

4

Living Presence of mercy,
    gently chiding us for blaming others and for hating
        ourselves,
take from our eyes the dust that blinds us,
that we may treat one another
    by the light of your compassion.
We pray this after the pattern of Jesus
    and in the power of the Spirit.

5

Living Presence of justice and grace,
    calling us to the freedom of your city,
so shape our lives in the ways of your justice
    that we may become worthy of that citizenship
        that you give us for our maturing
            and for our growth in wisdom,
in the commonwealth of your people,
    in the communion of your saints,
    and in the fellowship of Yeshua the Just.

6

Living Presence, calling us to a daily death,
give us courage to bear the marks of our dying
    as you wean us from envy and greed,
that we may be content to travel light in the world,
    as we dismantle the stockpiles of weapons and possessions,
    in the Spirit of the One
    who had nowhere to lay his head.

The Sunday between 12 and 18 June

Kyries

We have judged others too harshly and thought ourselves superior to them.

We have judged ourselves too harshly and thought ourselves inferior to others.

We have refused to accept that there is no condemnation, only compassion, in God's heart.

Response/Canticle/Hymn/Reflection

The Third Commandment

You shall not dishonour the name of the Lord your God.
You shall worship God with awe and reverence.

To honour a name is to follow a way,
to love a strange Wisdom, folly to the worldly.
'I Am Who I Am' is hardly a name,
making no sense to our restless minds.
Beware of the seduction of certainties,
live with the questions, the paradoxes.
Accept with patience the unresolved in your hearts,
living with trust into the future unknown.

For our God cannot be grasped and controlled,
the name is forever beyond our reach.

Silence

You shall not dishonour the name of the Lord your God.
You shall worship God with awe and reverence.

Gospel Acclamation

Alleluia, alleluia, alleluia.
Alleluia, alleluia, alleluia.

A Proclaim the good news: God's domain is among you, it is very near.
B The kingdom of God is like a wild plant that takes over your ordered garden.
C Know yourselves forgiven, and love will be released in you.

Alleluia, alleluia, alleluia.

A reading from the Gospel according to Matthew/Mark/Luke
Alleluia, alleluia, alleluia.

A *Matthew 9.35 — 10.8 [9–23]*
B *Mark 4.26–34*
C *Luke 7.36 — 8.3*

Give glory to the living God.
Alleluia, alleluia, alleluia.
Unfold the Living Word for us today.

THE SUNDAY BETWEEN 12 AND 18 JUNE

Collects

Year A

Living Presence of communion,
    empowering us when we journey
        to bring living words and a healing touch
            to those who give us shelter,
    and empowering us when we are at home
        to receive our guests with generous hospitality,
so that we may learn to love one another
    in a mutual giving and receiving of gifts,
renew this way of life and fellowship among us,
    that we may know, even in miniature,
    what it means to live in your domain.
We pray this after the pattern of Jesus
    and in the power of the Spirit.

Year B

Living Presence, unpredictable, disturbing,
    comparing your domain
        to the wild mustard plant
            that threatens what we cultivate so carefully,
may your seeds grow in us
    until we are strong enough
        to challenge those ordered worldly ways
            we take for granted,
that the unnoticed among us may at last grow tall,
    and take their place with dignity and worth.
We pray this after the pattern of Jesus
    and in the power of the Spirit.

THE SUNDAY BETWEEN 12 AND 18 JUNE

Year C

Living Presence of overflowing love,
    generous in forgiveness,
clear the arteries of our hardened hearts
    that we may no longer condemn others,
but, with them, trust ourselves to one another
    in your merciful embrace.
We pray this after the pattern of Jesus
    and in the power of the Spirit.

4

Living Presence of precise discernment,
    deftly and quickly probing the diseased heart of the world
        and dissolving the evil that is encrusted there,
heal our wounds
    and rescue us from all that traps us,
that we may no longer act in oppressive ways
    but set one another free,
after the pattern of the One
    who brought liberation and meaning to humankind.

5

Living Presence,
    whose love has been betrayed and denied
        over and over again,
    and whose covenants have been torn apart,
forgive our lack of trust and loyalty,
    and call us to yourself again,
we who bear the marks of Judas and of Cain.

THE SUNDAY BETWEEN 12 AND 18 JUNE

6

Living Presence of awesome wisdom,
   whose holiness sears and scours us,
harness the seething power of our anger,
   the whirlpools of rage,
   the waves of indignation,
and channel this awesome energy
   into the clear thoughts and passionate deeds
     that weave the patterns of justice among us,
   the justice that reconciles and restores,
     relentless and gentle, discerning and wise,
in the Spirit of Yeshua the Just,
   in whose name
     and in the power of whose Spirit we pray.

The Sunday between 19 and 25 June

Kyries

We have sometimes laughed at others rather than with them.

We have scowled when we might have smiled.

We have taken ourselves too seriously.

Response/Canticle/Hymn/Reflection

The Fourth Commandment

Remember the Sabbath
and keep it holy.
Christ is risen from the dead:
set your minds on that which endures,
not on the things that are passing away.

Set aside time out of time,
to rest and to be, to celebrate and to laugh.
Be thankful for small deeds of kindness,
as well as for the greatest of blessings.
Fill the past with the spirit of gratitude,
the future with the spirit of trust.

Silence

THE SUNDAY BETWEEN 19 AND 25 JUNE

Remember the Sabbath
and keep it holy.
Christ is risen from the dead:
set your minds on that which endures,
not on the things that are passing away.

Gospel Acclamation

Alleluia, alleluia, alleluia.
Alleluia, alleluia, alleluia.

A Hang on to your life and you will lose it. Let go of your life and you will find it.
B At the heart of the storm there is a calm abiding Presence.
C Do not be afraid to tell of all that God has done for you.

Alleluia, alleluia, alleluia.

A reading from the Gospel according to Matthew/Mark/Luke
Alleluia, alleluia, alleluia.

A Matthew 10.24–39
B Mark 4.35–41
C Luke 8.26–39

Give glory to the living God.
Alleluia, alleluia, alleluia.
Unfold the Living Word for us today.

THE SUNDAY BETWEEN 19 AND 25 JUNE

Collects

Year A

Loving Presence,
   vulnerable yet never defeated,
give us courage to emerge from the defences
   which we build for our security,
and give us the trust to surrender ourselves
   to your infinite care,
that we may be content with what is sufficient for today.
We pray this after the pattern of Jesus
   and in the power of the Spirit.

Year B

Living Presence of the peace which is beyond our grasp,
   refusing to let us escape from all that troubles us,
give us courage to enter the darkness of the storm
that we may discover there the stillness
   of your abiding presence.
We pray this after the pattern of Jesus
   and in the power of the Spirit.

Year C

Living Presence of liberation,
   working your power
     among the legions of destructive might
     and the demons of inner disturbance,
release us from our fears,
   protect us from everything that could overwhelm us,
   and bring all the powers of this present age
     to serve your just and gentle rule.
We pray this after the pattern of Jesus
   and in the power of the Spirit.

THE SUNDAY BETWEEN 19 AND 25 JUNE

4

Loving Presence,
  seeking always to create anew,
    even from the heart of evil, pain, and death,
  sustaining life in all your creatures,
    and present with them in their distress,
hold us lest we fall beyond your reach,
  and raise us by forgiveness and healing
    to a new love for one another and for you.
We pray this after the pattern of Jesus
  and in the power of the Spirit.

5

Living Presence, insistent, implacable,
  facing us with the truth
    that we have no power of ourselves to help ourselves,
raise us from the depths of exhaustion and despair,
  that we may be renewed with the energy of life and hope.
We pray this after the pattern of Jesus
  and in the power of the Spirit.

6

Living Presence of sharp laser and gently warming fire,
  revealing to us everything of which we are unaware,
expose the unrecognized devices of our murky hearts,
  the untapped resources of generosity and laughter,
  our unrealized capacity for truth and forbearance,
that we may know our true selves,
  and be reassured by the true humanity
    of Yeshua the Just,
after whose pattern
  and in whose Spirit we pray.

The Sunday between 26 June and 2 July

Kyries

We have claimed to do what is right
but we have not actually done it.

We have claimed and done what is right
but from outer obedience to the rules
and not from inner promptings of the heart.

We have claimed and done what is right,
both outwardly and inwardly,
but we have done these things by human power
and not by divine grace.

[Slightly adapted from J.D.Crossan and Jonathan Reed,
In Search of Paul*]*

Response/Canticle/Hymn/Reflection

The Fifth Commandment

Honour your father and your mother.
Live as servants of God:
let us work for the good of all,
especially members of the household of faith.

THE SUNDAY BETWEEN 26 JUNE AND 2 JULY

Let us live into the commitments we are given,
steadfast in caring for those we did not choose.
Let us face our lies and betrayals,
finding courage and truth within and between us.
Let us delve ever deeper the mines of forgiveness and trust,
touching with gentleness, our hearts full of compassion.

Silence

Honour your father and your mother.
Live as servants of God:
let us work for the good of all,
especially members of the household of faith.

Gospel Acclamation

Alleluia, alleluia, alleluia.
Alleluia, alleluia, alleluia.

A Let the spirit of welcome dwell in your heart.
B Receive the healing touch of the Gospel and its life-giving *power*.
C Hear the call, Follow me. Never look back.

Alleluia, alleluia, alleluia.

A reading from the Gospel according to Matthew/Mark/Luke
Alleluia, alleluia, alleluia.

A *Matthew 10.40–42*
B *Mark 5.21–43*
C *Luke 9.51–62*

Give glory to the living God.
Alleluia, alleluia, alleluia.
Unfold the Living Word for us today.

THE SUNDAY BETWEEN 26 JUNE AND 2 JULY

Collects

Year A

Faithful Presence,
  whose promises we often doubt
  and to whom we are often disloyal,
touch us in the midst of our perplexities,
that we may be reassured
  that in the simplest of kindly acts,
    given and received,
  your covenant is sustained.
We pray this after the pattern of Jesus
  and in the power of the Spirit.

Year B

Constant Presence, life-giving and life-restoring,
  liberating and healing us
    through the words of wisdom
    and through the touch and skills
      of those who draw close to us,
alert us to the gifts that come to us day by day,
  if we will but open ourselves
    to receive them in trust.
We pray this after the pattern of Jesus
  and in the power of the Spirit.

Year C

Determined Presence of tough and enduring love,
  whose stern care for our greatest good
    warns us of the siren songs of worldly security,
strengthen us to follow your way alone,
  and to trust that the loss of goods or honour or life itself
    can never separate us from your presence.
We pray this after the pattern of Jesus
  and in the power of the Spirit.

THE SUNDAY BETWEEN 26 JUNE AND 2 JULY

4

Living Presence of freedom,
   holding out to us the gift of the keys,
unlock the hearts and minds and wills of your people
   who strive to be human in the city,
that your love may cast out fear,
   and that we may know again
      that we belong to one another and to you.
We pray this after the pattern of Jesus
   and in the power of the Spirit.

5

Living Presence,
   faithful to your covenants,
   loyal to your people,
deepen our trust in your promises,
   and our faithfulness in our response,
that your loving purposes for humankind may be realized,
   and not one of us come to lasting harm.
We pray this after the pattern of Jesus
   and in the power of the Spirit.

6

Living Presence of wisdom,
   revealing the paradox of power and weakness,
   trusting into our hands enormous power for good or ill,
   power that we struggle to understand and use aright,
set before us again the ways of Yeshua
   and work through us in your Spirit,
that we may steward our planet carefully,
   and guard and guide whoever and whatever
      is entrusted to our care,

that we may not bind or throttle others,
  but free them to take their place
    and claim their share
  in the inheritance you have given us.
We pray this after the pattern of Jesus
  and in the power of the Spirit.

The Sunday between 3 and 9 July

Kyries

We have become bloated balloons: puncture us.

We have become full of ourselves: empty us.

We have missed one another by miles: focus us.

Response/Canticle/Hymn/Reflection

The Sixth Commandment

You shall not commit murder.
Reverence all life.
Live at peace with everyone:
overcome evil with good.

Take your neighbour to your heart;
welcome the stranger in your midst.
Be generous and hospitable,
with your time, round your table.
Deepen your respect, one for another,
receive your guests as you would wish to be received.

Silence

THE SUNDAY BETWEEN 3 AND 9 JULY

You shall not commit murder.
Reverence all life.
Live at peace with everyone:
overcome evil with good.

Gospel Acclamation

Alleluia, alleluia, alleluia.
Alleluia, alleluia, alleluia.

A Hear of the yoke that is easy, the burden that is light.
B Listen to the prophets, without honour among those who know them well.
C Proclaim the good news: God's domain is among you, it is very near.

Alleluia, alleluia, alleluia.

A reading from the Gospel according to Matthew/Mark/Luke
Alleluia, alleluia, alleluia.

A *Matthew 11.16–19, 25–30*
B *Mark 6.1–13*
C *Luke 10.1–11, 16–20*

Give glory to the living God.
Alleluia, alleluia, alleluia.
Unfold the Living Word for us today.

THE SUNDAY BETWEEN 3 AND 9 JULY

Collects

Year A

Living Presence, folly to worldly ways,
   just and compassionate in your rule,
   revealing the strength of love
     by being born a vulnerable child
     and by dying a nailtorn outcast,
turn our eyes and desires
   from the seductions and trappings of worldly power,
and give us the strength
   to risk being vulnerable ourselves,
that we may learn how to become
   truly wise and divinely human.
We pray this after the pattern of Jesus
   and in the power of the Spirit.

Year B

Living Presence of wisdom and discernment,
   whose prophets recognize the inconvenient truths,
give them courage
   to say what they know will disturb us,
and give us steady hearts and wills
   to listen to what they say
   and to act upon it.
We pray this after the pattern of Jesus
   and in the power of the Spirit.

Year C

Living Presence of extraordinary love,
   revealing your nature to us
     when you are most vulnerable, defenceless, and naked,
clear from our lives all that keeps us defended from the truth,
   possessions, clothes, words, and fears,

that we may recognize one another
   as sisters and brothers in your love.
We pray this after the pattern of Jesus
   and in the power of the Spirit.

4

Living Presence to Abraham and Sarah,
   our ancestors in faith,
      calling us to journey through the desert to your city,
take the energy of our prayers and deeds
   and transform our cities into places of pilgrimage and peace
      for all who arrive there tired and hungry.
We pray this after the pattern of Jesus
   and in the power of the Spirit.

5

Living Presence of truth,
   giving us the spirit of resistance to the subtleties of evil,
   insinuating themselves as we grow stronger on the journey,
may we be honest pilgrims,
   steadfast, trustworthy, and true of heart,
   rooted only in your love.
We pray this in the Spirit of Jesus,
   the pioneer of the new and living way.

6

Living Pioneer,
   always ahead of us on the pilgrim journey,
   drawing us to the places that focus your presence,
      to Ynys Enlli/Bardsey Island and to Lindisfarne,
      to Iona and to Durham, to Canterbury and to Jerusalem,
      to Santiago and to Rome,
inspire us to take courage from our ancestors of faith,
   to make sacred the places where we live now,
   and to let ourselves be made holy
      in the Spirit of the One who has pioneered the living Way.

The Sunday between 10 and 16 July

Kyries

We have not cleared our homes of clutter.

We keep replaying our inner tape of chatter.

We have filled the airwaves with too much clatter.

Response/Canticle/Hymn/Reflection

The Seventh Commandment

You shall not commit adultery.
You shall not betray the one to whom you are promised.
Know that your body is a temple of the Holy Spirit.
Give and receive without reserve.

Honour each other and always be kind:
do not let the sun go down on your wrath.
Let the other challenge your selfishness:
true love is tough and takes time to mature.
Do all you can for the other's well-being,
honour the other as the place of God's dwelling.
Be loyal to each other, full of faith in each other,
unfolding the promise your life-day long.

Silence

You shall not commit adultery.
You shall not betray the one to whom you are promised.
Know that your body is a temple of the Holy Spirit.
Give and receive without reserve.

Gospel Acclamation

Alleluia, alleluia, alleluia.
Alleluia, alleluia, alleluia.

- A Hear the word; understand; and yield much fruit.
- B Take courage and tell truth to power.
- C Let your enemy love you.

Alleluia, alleluia, alleluia.

A reading from the Gospel according to Matthew/Mark/Luke
Alleluia, alleluia, alleluia.

- A *Matthew 13.1–9, 18–23*
- B *Mark 6.14–29*
- C *Luke 10.25–37*

Give glory to the living God.
Alleluia, alleluia, alleluia.
Unfold the Living Word for us today.

THE SUNDAY BETWEEN 10 AND 16 JULY

Collects

Year A

Living Presence, quiet, hidden,
   sowing the seed within us in great hope,
may we not reject it through hardness of heart,
but let it take root
   so that we may be
      strong enough to bear with troubles,
      discerning enough to resist the lures of security,
      and patient enough to give the time for ripening,
to the good of others and to our own lasting joy.
We pray this after the pattern of Jesus
   and in the power of the Spirit.

Year B

Living Presence of righteousness,
   whose peace does not come
      in the worldly ways of violence and victory,
      but in the heavenly ways of truth and justice,
give us steadfast hearts
   to refuse the broad, well-trodden path of force
   and to clear and follow the narrow path of patient persistence
      that leads to reconciliation.
We pray this after the pattern of Jesus
   and in the power of the Spirit.

Year C

Living Presence of demanding love,
   making yourself vulnerable even to your enemies,
   revealing yourself to us in the most unlikely faces,
give us courage when we are needy,

that we may trust the approach of those
   whom we have been taught to reject
   and who make us tremble with fear.
We pray this after the pattern of Jesus
   and in the power of the Spirit.

4

Breather of the air,
   gentle in the breeze, beautiful in voice and word,
move among us
   in the wordless cries of creation
   and in the shaped voices of human beings,
that the sighs of each heart
   and the sounds of faithful lips
may be joined in a harmony of exultant joy,
   in one another and in you,
revealed to us through the mouth of Jesus
   and in the wind of the Spirit.

5

Living Presence of wonder,
   ceaselessly creating and restoring,
astonish us with your generosity
   and still our hearts in awe and wonder.
We pray this after the pattern of Jesus
   and in the power of the Spirit.

6

Living Presence of our ancestors' faith,
   fading from view as our own sight grows dim,
continue your work in us and through all the world,
   until our eyes open to a strange and shocking light,
   a scarcely believable new dawn.
We pray this after the pattern of Jesus
   and in the power of the Spirit.

The Sunday between 17 and 23 July

Kyries

We are often beside ourselves and do not live from deep within ourselves.

We are so easily pulled out of our true orbit.

We lose touch with the still centre of our being.

Response/Canticle/Hymn/Reflection

The Eighth Commandment

You shall not steal.
Be honest in all that you do
and care for those in need.

Whatever unexpectedly comes your way,
pass it on to those in greater need than your own.
Resist the temptation to hoard,
simplify your life and lighten your load.
Contribute to the common good of your community,
to the good of the world, whatever it costs.
Reverence the earth
and replenish what you have taken.

Silence

THE SUNDAY BETWEEN 17 AND 23 JULY

You shall not steal.
**Be honest in all that you do
and care for those in need.**

Gospel Acclamation

Alleluia, alleluia, alleluia.
Alleluia, alleluia, alleluia.

A   Let no words of condemnation fall from your lips.
B   Touch but the hem of his coat and you will be well.
C   Listen, and let the word of stillness calm your anxieties.

Alleluia, alleluia, alleluia.

A reading from the Gospel according to Matthew/Mark/Luke
Alleluia, alleluia, alleluia.

A   *Matthew 13.24–30, 36–43*
B   *Mark 6.30–34, 53–56*
C   *Luke 10.38–42*

Give glory to the living God.
Alleluia, alleluia, alleluia.
Unfold the Living Word for us today.

THE SUNDAY BETWEEN 17 AND 23 JULY

Collects

Year A

God of discerning and compassionate judgement,
   never absent from any human being,
   and seeing deeper than we can ever do
      into the chasms of the human heart,
deliver us from self-righteousness,
   transform our bitter and judgemental minds,
   and give us your spirit of patient endurance.
We pray this after the pattern of Jesus
   and in the power of the Spirit.

Year B

Living Presence, wise and discerning,
   to whom we cry for help when everything around us
      crumbles,
meet our needs in ways we cannot predict,
   and touch us in the depths of our being,
   where, cure or not,
   your healing presence assures us that all shall be well.
We pray this after the pattern of Jesus
   and in the power of the Spirit.

Year C

Living Presence of the still small voice,
   creating a pool of calm in the midst of the storm,
awaken in the depths of our being
   such a sense of your presence
that we may lay aside all anxiety and fuss.
We pray this after the pattern of Jesus
   and in the power of the Spirit.

THE SUNDAY BETWEEN 17 AND 23 JULY

4

Living Presence of fire,
   refining us in the truth, and warming us with love,
burn all that is impure with the laser beam of clarity,
and with gentle flame stir into life the frozen battered child
   who longs to yawn and stretch, run free and live again.
We pray this after the pattern of Jesus
   and in the power of the Spirit.

5

Lion of wrath,
   prowling in love for us,
   relentlessly padding after us,
from whom our familiar false selves cower in fear,
   slinking back into the cages
      we have made for ourselves,
give us courage to turn and face you,
   in the white heat of your love melt our iron bars,
   and in one bound rescue us despite ourselves.
We pray this after the pattern of Jesus
   and in the power of the Spirit.

6

Rescuer, Liberator,
   yearning for us to realize how trapped we are,
   giving us freedom to choose to be imprisoned,
   yet compelling us with your insistent love,
turn our hearts and wills without our knowing it,
   and kindle in us both the desire for true freedom
   and the courage to bear it,
that we may know ourselves delivered
   in love's most costly way,
      at one with Yeshua,
      for whom such love was the weight of glory.

The Sunday between 24 and 30 July

Kyries

We react to what is urgent rather than respond to what is important.

We are easily distracted from our true purpose.

We are distracted from distraction by distractions.

Response/Canticle/Hymn/Reflection

The Ninth Commandment

You shall not be a false witness.
Let everyone speak the truth.

Beware the white lies that you easily tell,
lest even your kindness lead you astray.
Learn to speak the truth with tact,
do not be brutal in your honesty.
Do not be trapped in a web of deceit,
let the bracing truth set you free.
Tell the stories that have harmed you and shamed you,
choosing a listener who will not betray you.

Silence

You shall not be a false witness.
Let everyone speak the truth.

THE SUNDAY BETWEEN 24 AND 30 JULY

Gospel Acclamation

Alleluia, alleluia, alleluia.
Alleluia, alleluia, alleluia.

A   Bring out of your treasure what is new and what is old.
B   Gather the fragments, that nothing may be lost.
C   Ask and it will be given you.

Alleluia, alleluia, alleluia.

A reading from the Gospel according to Matthew/John/Luke
Alleluia, alleluia, alleluia.

A   *Matthew 13.31–33, 44–52*
B   *John 6.1–21*
C   *Luke 11.1–13*

Give glory to the living God.
Alleluia, alleluia, alleluia.
Unfold the Living Word for us today.

Collects

Year A

Mysterious hidden Presence,
   concealed in parable, paradox, and riddle,
disturb our comfort,
   question what we take for granted,
     challenge the assumptions
       by which we usually live,
and so reveal to us the secret of your domain.
We pray this after the pattern of Jesus
   and in the power of the Spirit.

THE SUNDAY BETWEEN 24 AND 30 JULY

Year B

Living Presence of abundance,
   feeding us when we are hungry,
   calming us when we are afraid,
meet us in our need when we least expect it,
and renew our trust in your providence,
   day by day.
We pray this after the pattern of Jesus
   and in the power of the Spirit.

Year C

Living Presence, overflowing with generosity,
   always more willing to give than we to ask,
raise our eyes and lift our hearts
   to embrace the wonder of your love,
and give us what we most deeply desire,
   even that which we do not yet know that we need.
We pray this after the pattern of Jesus
   and in the power of the Spirit.

4

Living Presence, puzzling and perplexing,
   justify your ways to your people,
   and let not our cry for justice echo in silence,
so that, as we cling to our trust in your promises,
   we may know they have been fulfilled,
   that we have not been betrayed,
   and that you are not false, but true.
We pray this after the pattern of Jesus
   and in the power of the Spirit.

THE SUNDAY BETWEEN 24 AND 30 JULY

5

Living Presence of glory and splendour,
  whose bright radiance we see in glimpses of wonder,
  both rare and everyday,
open our eyes and our hearts,
  alert the nerve ends of our being,
that in trembling and rapture
  all our fears may dissolve in your presence.
We pray this in the name of the One
  who is the light of the world.

6

Living Presence of unusual power,
  compassionate and just,
  wielder of the one sword
    that pierces with truth and healing,
penetrate the murk and fury of our hearts,
that our anger may be shaped
  by the example of Jesus
  and by the power of your Spirit,
that we may create with you
  the commonwealth of justice and peace
    for which we pray, yours with us,
    on earth as it is in heaven.

The Sunday between 31 July and 6 August

Kyries

We have betrayed our humanity by thinking of others or ourselves as destined for dust rather than for glory.

We have not brought the light of transfiguration into dark places.

We have not listened to the wisdom of the divinely human One, transfigured on the mountain.

Response/Canticle/Hymn/Reflection

The Tenth Commandment

You shall not covet anything which belongs to your neighbour.
Remember the words of the Lord Jesus:
It is more blessed to give than to receive.
Love your neighbour as yourself,
for love is the fulfilling of the law.

Confront the envy and greed in your heart,
all that is killing your ability to love.
Be generous with your gifts and your time,
give of your skills to help those in need.
Graciously receive the smallest of gifts,
worthless in the market, priceless to you.

THE SUNDAY BETWEEN 31 JULY AND 6 AUGUST

Refuse the burden of a safe that will crush you:
throw away the keys and the codes.
Let a beautiful shell picked up from the beach
be a sacrament of friends remembered for ever.

Silence

You shall not covet anything which belongs to your neighbour.
Remember the words of the Lord Jesus:
It is more blessed to give than to receive.
Love your neighbour as yourself,
for love is the fulfilling of the law.

Gospel Acclamation

Alleluia, alleluia, alleluia.
Alleluia, alleluia, alleluia.

A   Bring what you have and give them something to eat.
B   Thus says the Living One: Put your trust in the One whom I have sent.
C   Your life does not consist of possessions. Be rich toward God.

Alleluia, alleluia, alleluia.

A reading from the Gospel according to Matthew/John/Luke
Alleluia, alleluia, alleluia.

A   *Matthew 14.13–21*
B   *John 6.24–35*
C   *Luke 12.13–21*

Give glory to the living God.
Alleluia, alleluia, alleluia.
Unfold the Living Word for us today.

THE SUNDAY BETWEEN 31 JULY AND 6 AUGUST

Collects

In connection with the Feast of the Transfiguration on the 6th August, see the prayers for the Sunday before Lent, and prayers 4 & 5 in the week following this one.

Year A

Living Presence, persuasive, generous,
   opening reluctant hearts,
   prising clenched fists apart,
fill us with the spiritual food of compassion
   and a willingness to share,
and renew in us the conviction
   that together we can more than meet
      one another's needs for daily bread.
We pray this after the pattern of Jesus
   and in the power of the Spirit.

Year B

Living Presence,
   revealed to us as the bread of life,
so sustain us with your daily manna
   that we may learn to trust
      that you will feed us in every corner of our being,
         satisfying what we most deeply desire.
We pray this after the pattern of Jesus
   and in the power of the Spirit.

THE SUNDAY BETWEEN 31 JULY AND 6 AUGUST

Year C

Living Presence of abundant life,
    pruning us of excess and greed,
show us again that to accumulate is to wither,
    and to distribute is to thrive,
that through us your kingdom may come on earth.
We pray this after the pattern of Jesus
    and in the power of the Spirit.

4

Living Presence, affirming our dignity,
    take from us the burden of self-hatred,
    the whisper of loathing
        that says we are worthless,
and fill us with the spirit of welcome and grace,
that we may deeply accept
    that we are accepted as we are,
in the companionship of Jesus,
    beloved of your heart.

5

Mysterious Presence, fierce and tender,
    whose searing love reaches out
        even to those who cause most harm,
bring into the light of day our half-truths,
    our whispers and our rumours,
brand our hearts with a great love for our enemies,
    even those who brazenly lie
    and imprison the tellers of truth,
that our love for them may turn their hearts,
so shedding on them and us the painful healing beams
    of the light of Jesus, the Way, the Truth, and the Life.

THE SUNDAY BETWEEN 31 JULY AND 6 AUGUST

6

Living Presence of love and liberation,
   scraping from our hearts our apathy and fear,
so fill us with courage
   that we may give passionately of ourselves,
      in solidarity with the destitute and the oppressed,
that together we may find our freedom
   in the service of your just and gentle rule.
We pray this after the pattern of Jesus
   and in the power of the Spirit.

The Sunday between 7 and 13 August

Kyries

We have let the diabolical divide us from one another and from our true selves.

We have let fear separate us from those who want to give us love.

We have lost our sense of spiritual direction and wander about in muddle and fog.

Response/Canticle/Hymn/Reflection

The Promise of Solitude and Solidarity

Follow the ancient path of chastity,
call upon the faith of your forebears.
It is the way of affection and goodwill,
love's promise, love's narrow way,
a way of hope, to be taken to heart,
to be lived from the heart.
Gently but firmly lay aside all lust,
the temptation to dominate by physical power,
the battering of force,
the craving for control.
Go through the narrow gate of loneliness,
the heart's hollowing, letting others be.

THE SUNDAY BETWEEN 7 AND 13 AUGUST

So we shall come to the place of solitude and solidarity,
of joyful communion and love.

Gospel Acclamation

Alleluia, alleluia, alleluia.
Alleluia, alleluia, alleluia.

A Take heart: it is I. Do not be afraid.
B Eat of the living bread and you will know eternal life.
C Make ready to meet God's unexpected moment.

Alleluia, alleluia, alleluia.

A reading from the Gospel according to Matthew/John/Luke
Alleluia, alleluia, alleluia.

A *Matthew 14.22–33*
B *John 6.35,41–51*
C *Luke 12.32–40*

Give glory to the living God.
Alleluia, alleluia, alleluia.
Unfold the Living Word for us today.

Collects

Year A

Living Presence, ever-faithful and reliable,
 bulwark in the storm,
in the midst of our doubts
 shore up our faltering trust,
that we may be raised up in hope
 even when we think we are drowning in despair.

We pray this after the pattern of Jesus
   and in the power of the Spirit.

Year B

Living Presence, nurturing Householder,
   baking the living bread,
feed us when we no longer know how to find sustenance,
that our strength may be renewed,
   and that our feet may take us
      further than we have so far journeyed,
      further than we ever imagined we should have to go.
We pray this after the pattern of Jesus
   and in the power of the Spirit.

Year C

Living Presence, awesome in being so vulnerable,
   stripping us of all that seems to make us secure,
      money, health, and life itself,
give us courage to face you
   as we were when we were born,
      naked, vulnerable, defenceless,
      saved only by love,
      even at midnight's hour.
We pray this after the pattern of Jesus
   and in the power of the Spirit.

THE SUNDAY BETWEEN 7 AND 13 AUGUST

4 (on or near 7 August)

Living Presence of radiant light,
  whose face no one can look upon and live,
sustain our faith in the human face of Christ,
  revealing the infinite depths of your justice and compassion,
and so shine upon us the light of your Spirit
  that we may recognize you in the faces of one another,
  and realize the presence of your glory among us.
We pray this in the Spirit of the Transfigured One,
  who is the Light of the world.

5 (on or near 8 August)

Living Presence of light and love,
  shining in the darkest depths of our hearts
  and to the utmost bounds of the universe,
illuminate the whole creation,
  that all things, seen and unseen,
  may be transfigured to glory.
We pray this in and through the Spirit of Yeshua,
  radiant in the splendour of the wounds of love.

6

Transforming Presence,
  looking upon us with eyes of compassion,
  call us with the word of forgiveness,
    again and again, to seventy times seven,
that we may at last hear and see,
  and turn our stricken and wounded faces
  to your transfiguring light,
that we may know ourselves accepted and embraced,
  loved beyond measure and without reserve.
We pray this after the pattern of Jesus
  and in the power of the Spirit.

The Sunday between 14 and 20 August

Kyries

We have been sluggish and not learned from the ants.

We have been prey to the deadly sin of sloth.

We have slumped in laziness before the television, our favourite idol.

Response/Canticle/Hymn/Reflection

The Promise of Simplicity and Spaciousness

Follow the ancient path of poverty,
call upon the faith of your forebears.
It is the way of nakedness and generosity,
freedom's promise, freedom's narrow way,
a way of hope, to be taken to heart,
to be lived from the heart.
Gently but firmly lay aside all rust,
the temptation to dominate by the power of money,
the cluttering of things,
the craving for comfort.
Go through the narrow gate of constriction,
the heart's hollowing, letting possessions go.
So we shall come to the place of simplicity and spaciousness,
of glad conviviality and freedom.

THE SUNDAY BETWEEN 14 AND 20 AUGUST

Gospel Acclamation

Alleluia, alleluia, alleluia.
Alleluia, alleluia, alleluia.

A   Great is your faith! Let it be done for you as you wish.
B   Feed on the living bread that came down from heaven.
C   Do you know how to interpret the present time?

Alleluia, alleluia, alleluia.

A reading from the Gospel according to Matthew/John/Luke
Alleluia, alleluia, alleluia.

A   *Matthew 15. (10–20) 21–28*
B   *John 6.51–58*
C   *Luke 12.49–56*

Give glory to the living God.
Alleluia, alleluia, alleluia.
Unfold the Living Word for us today.

Collects

Year A

Living Presence, welcoming and vulnerable,
   stretching the boundaries of our compassion,
give us courage to see you in every face we meet,
   however strange,
that our fear may melt
   when the face in front of us is threatening.
We pray this after the pattern of Jesus
   and in the power of the Spirit.

THE SUNDAY BETWEEN 14 AND 20 AUGUST

Year B

Living Presence of compassion,
    living the life of the wanderer upon earth,
    always dependent on the generosity of others,
touch us again in the places of our being
    where we are starving and destitute,
        with no power of ourselves to help ourselves,
that you may teach us that all is yours,
    all indeed is gift.
We pray this after the pattern of Jesus
    and in the power of the Spirit.

Year C

Mysterious Presence,
    dividing us from one another
        to bring the truth to light,
            searing in its judgement,
move also among us now
    with your reconciling power,
that our love may be deepened
    and our communion enriched.
We pray this after the pattern of Jesus
    and in the power of the Spirit.

4

Living Presence of compassion and friendship,
    warming the frozen places of our fears,
    irrigating the deserts of our apathy,
dismantle the wall around our pain and loss,
    and lift the burdens of our past,
that we may be free to live in trust with one another,
    and in the joy of your presence
        build at least the tents of justice.
We pray this after the pattern of Jesus
    and in the power of the Spirit.

5

Living Presence, infinitely caring and tactful,
    raining showers of gentleness upon us,
give us grace to be kind to one another,
    and also to ourselves,
that compassion may rule in our hearts,
and that we may have courage to approach
    even those who have betrayed us,
and in the Spirit of the One who harrows hell,
    greet them with a kiss.

6

Living Presence, full of promise,
    holding before us what we can barely imagine,
    and what we see but fleetingly fulfilled,
keep our hope alive,
    and hasten the day
        when we shall know the promise has been kept.
We pray this after the pattern of Jesus
    and in the power of the Spirit.

The Sunday between 21 and 27 August

Kyries

We tell lies to avoid being found out.

We blame others and make them suffer unjustly.

We sell our true selves to save our face.

Response/Canticle/Hymn/Reflection

The Promise of Silence and Stillness

Follow the ancient path of obedience,
call upon the faith of your forebears.
It is the way of listening and truthfulness,
wisdom's promise, wisdom's narrow way,
a way of hope, to be taken to heart,
to be lived from the heart.
Gently but firmly lay aside all fuss,
the temptation to dominate by the power of words,
the clattering of noise,
the craving for certainty.
Go through the narrow gate of not knowing,
the heart's hollowing, letting words go.
So we shall come to the place of silence and stillness,
of true conversation and wisdom.

THE SUNDAY BETWEEN 21 AND 27 AUGUST

Gospel Acclamation

Alleluia, alleluia, alleluia.
Alleluia, alleluia, alleluia.

A   Who do you say that Jesus is?
B   Will you also turn away? To whom else will you go?
C   Meet the needs of those in pain: do not turn away.

Alleluia, alleluia, alleluia.

A reading from the Gospel according to Matthew/John/Luke
Alleluia, alleluia, alleluia.

A   Matthew 16.13–20
B   John 6.56–69
C   Luke 13.10–17

Give glory to the living God.
Alleluia, alleluia, alleluia.
Unfold the Living Word for us today.

Collects

Year A

Living Presence, strangely powerful,
   emptying yourself in Jesus your beloved,
   giving yourself into the hands of those you have created,
   entrusting human beings with the power to bind
     and the power to loosen,
give us the wisdom that we so desperately need,
   to discern when to restrain and when to liberate,
that we may draw closer to one another
   in your searing and healing love.
We pray this after the pattern of Jesus
   and in the power of the Spirit.

THE SUNDAY BETWEEN 21 AND 27 AUGUST

Year B

Living Presence,
   whose Word comes alive in our hearts,
   disturbing us with questions
      for which we have no answers,
draw us closer to one another as the Body of Christ,
that we may find there the truest word,
   of timeless life and unexpected glory.
We pray this after the pattern of Jesus
   and in the power of the Spirit.

Year C

Living Presence, persistent, persevering,
   again and again bringing before our eyes
      our neighbours with their troubles,
irrigate the dried-up channels of our compassion
   with your living water,
that we may not be distracted from human need
   by religious habit or by self-centred concern.
We pray this after the pattern of Jesus
   and in the power of the Spirit.

4

Living Presence of infinite patience,
   calming our turbulent hearts,
take from us the stress of seeking for security
   in force of arms and luxury of comfort,
that we may know the quiet confidence
   of those who have enough for today
   and are learning to trust you for tomorrow.
We pray this after the pattern of Jesus
   and in the power of the Spirit.

THE SUNDAY BETWEEN 21 AND 27 AUGUST

5

Living Presence, patient, persistent,
  woven into the very fabric of the universe,
  for ever committed to bringing harmony out of chaos,
assure us of your presence
  in the midst of our perplexities and fears,
that you will endure with us
  and work the calm continuing way
    of a deeper and more lasting peace.
We pray this after the pattern of Jesus
  and in the power of the Spirit.

6

Living Presence, reconciling and restoring,
  whose heart is wrung by the cries of those who suffer
    injustice,
work in us and through us
  new deeds of discerning wisdom and true judgement,
that we may know among us the fufilment of your promises,
  according to your wisdom and your justice,
after the pattern of Jesus
  and in the power of the Spirit.

The Sunday between 28 August and 3 September

Kyries

We are often whitewashed tombs.

Our institutions are often cancerous within.

Only the surface is left, and there is nothing underneath.

Response/Canticle/Hymn/Reflection

The Way of Love: 1 Love's Persistence

Love is patient and kind
and knows no envy.
Love never clings,
is never boastful, conceited, or rude.
Love is never selfish,
never insists on its own way.
Love is not quick to take offence.
Love keeps no score of wrongs.
Love does not gloat over the sins of others.
Love rejoices in the truth.
Love is tough;
there is nothing it cannot face.
Love never loses trust
in human beings or in God.

THE SUNDAY BETWEEN 28 AUGUST AND 3 SEPTEMBER

Love never loses hope, never loses heart.
Love still stands when all else has fallen.
Faith, hope, and love abide, these three:
it is love that crowns them all.

Gospel Acclamation

Alleluia, alleluia, alleluia.
Alleluia, alleluia, alleluia.

A What profit is it to gain the whole world and lose your true being?
B Repent of the evil intentions in your hearts.
C Invite to your table those who are destitute, those who are stigmatized.

Alleluia, alleluia, alleluia.

A reading from the Gospel according to Matthew/Mark/Luke
Alleluia, alleluia, alleluia.

A *Matthew 16.21–28*
B *Mark 7.1–8, 14–15, 21–23*
C *Luke 14.1,7–14*

Give glory to the living God.
Alleluia, alleluia, alleluia.
Unfold the Living Word for us today.

THE SUNDAY BETWEEN 28 AUGUST AND 3 SEPTEMBER

Collects

Year A

Ever-creating God,
  blessing this earth and all that is in it,
keep us from the destitution
  of having nothing to cherish,
and from the excess
  that cherishes possessions
  rather than those who are in need.
We pray this after the pattern of Jesus
  and in the power of the Spirit.

Year B

Living Presence, wise and discerning,
  taking no account of appearances,
  but seeing deep into the human heart,
bring to our awareness
  the evil intentions that so often lurk unnoticed,
and before we have time to act upon them
  dissolve them in your goodness,
that we may always incline our hearts
  to serve your just and gentle rule.
We pray this after the pattern of Jesus
  and in the power of the Spirit.

THE SUNDAY BETWEEN 28 AUGUST AND 3 SEPTEMBER

Year C

Living Presence, open-hearted,
   generous and vulnerable,
      identifying with those we turn away from,
      with those we tread under our feet,
      with the nobodies of our world,
give us grace and courage to follow the One
   who took the lowest place,
   and who invited the destitute to the banquet,
that joy and laughter may be released
   into crabbed and barren lives.
We pray this after the pattern of Jesus
   and in the power of the Spirit.

4

Living, loving, holy Mystery,
   our joy resting in you and coming from you,
   making us content to be your people,
   humbled by your care for us,
give us courage to embody your will on earth,
that we may be loyal and steadfast, faithful and kind,
   trusting you for all that is to come.
We pray this after the pattern of Jesus
   and in the power of the Spirit.

THE SUNDAY BETWEEN 28 AUGUST AND 3 SEPTEMBER

5

Living Presence of truth,
  holding before our eyes
    a vision of your commonwealth,
  your rule of integrity and wisdom,
    justice and compassion,
give to those in public life
  minds that are true
    and hearts that are courageous,
that they may always be humbled by those who pass by,
  and always put the unnoticed first.
We pray this after the pattern of Jesus
  and in the power of the Spirit.

6

Living Presence of fierce and tender love,
  filling us with anger at the injustice
    that infects human life,
  yet clothing that anger with compassion,
may we never lose respect for human beings,
  each and all created in your image,
that we may overcome all desire to harm
  and all prejudice that treats others
    as less than human.
We pray this after the pattern of Jesus
  and in the power of the Spirit.

The Sunday between 4 and 10 September

Kyries

We are afraid of what the neighbours will say.

We are terrified of being humiliated by disgrace.

We have not let past hurts deepen our need for *God's* everlasting outstretched arms.

Response/Canticle/Hymn/Reflection

The Way of Love: 2 The Gospel Way

Let us love our enemies,
doing good to those who hate us.
Let us bless those who curse us,
and pray for those who abuse us.
Let us do good and lend,
expecting nothing in return.
For God is kind to the ungrateful and selfish.
Let us be merciful,
as God, like a good father, is merciful.
Let us not judge,
and we shall not be judged.

THE SUNDAY BETWEEN 4 AND 10 SEPTEMBER

Let us not condemn,
and we shall not be condemned.
Let us forgive,
and we shall be forgiven.
Let us give,
and gifts will be be given to us.
The measure we give
will be the measure we receive.

Gospel Acclamation

Alleluia, alleluia, alleluia.
Alleluia, alleluia, alleluia.

A   Do not let the sun set on your disputes: be reconciled to one another.
B   Speak the truth that you have never voiced before.
C   Whoever does not carry the cross and follow me cannot be my disciple.

Alleluia, alleluia, alleluia.

A reading from the Gospel according to Matthew/Mark/Luke
Alleluia, alleluia, alleluia.

A   *Matthew 18.15–20*
B   *Mark 7.24–37*
C   *Luke 14.25–33*

Give glory to the living God.
Alleluia, alleluia, alleluia.
Unfold the Living Word for us today.

THE SUNDAY BETWEEN 4 AND 10 SEPTEMBER

Collects

Year A

Living Presence of justice and compassion,
   seeking the greatest good of humankind,
keep our hearts and minds open to one another
   when we quarrel,
that we may respect and listen to those
   with whom we disagree,
that we may be humbled by the stories
   we have not heard before,
and that we may be moved to reconciliation
   and a new wisdom.
We pray this after the pattern of Jesus
   and in the power of the Spirit.

Year B

Living Presence, rescuing, liberating,
   opening ears and eyes and mouths,
release us from all that binds us,
that we may indeed hear your word
   and see your beauty,
and at last speak the truth with our own voice.
We pray this after the pattern of Jesus
   and in the power of the Spirit.

Year C

Loving Presence, stern, demanding,
   revealing to us the cost of true love,
deepen our awareness
   of how much you ask of us,
and fill us with the courage
   to give to others something that we hold dear.
We pray this after the pattern of Jesus
   and in the power of the Spirit.

THE SUNDAY BETWEEN 4 AND 10 SEPTEMBER

4

Mystery of divine love,
   in your covenants of grace and gifts
      binding us together with you,
   in the paradox of our free will and destiny
      moving through us as we embrace one another,
so enable us to choose in friendship
   to share our being and becoming,
that we fulfil our humanity
   by maturing in the ways of true love.
We pray this after the pattern of Jesus
   and in the power of the Spirit.

5

Living Presence of the promises of love,
   inspiring us to be steady and reliable in our loving,
give us courage and passion and steadfastness
   to live for the well-being of one another,
   to honour one another as your dwelling-place,
   and to be loyal, and full of faith in one another,
our life-day long.

6

Living Presence of the morning stars that sing together,
   inspiring us,
   welling up within our hearts,
   transforming us as we hear the melodies of grace,
fill our voices with the music
   of lament and celebration,
   of loyalty and questioning,
   of love and protest,
that we may be your partners
   in the weaving of the tapestries of glory.
We pray this after the pattern of Jesus
   and in the power of the Spirit.

The Sunday between 11 and 17 September

Kyries

Our defences are ingenious.

Our promises are bogus.

Our faces are but masks.

The first two lines are from Sogyal Rinpoche,
The Tibetan Book of Living and Dying

Response/Canticle/Hymn/Reflection

The Way of Love: 3 Dwelling in love

If we dwell in the divine love,
if we join the dance of the Lover,
the Beloved, and the Mutual Friend,
if we are caught up in the love
that is generous and overflowing,
we shall find ourselves loving and being loved
with the whole of our being,
loving our neighbours as ourselves,
and loving even our enemies.

And as surely as night follows day,
we shall never use force,
though we shall refuse to let others escape from love and truth;
we shall never use others merely to provide what we want,
though we shall acknowledge and respect our own needs;
we shall never take advantage of others' ignorance or
  immaturity –
though we shall try to increase their knowledge and wisdom.

Gospel Acclamation

Alleluia, alleluia, alleluia.
Alleluia, alleluia, alleluia.

A To seventy times seven forgive your sisters and brothers from your heart.
B Who do you say that Jesus is?
C Seek out the rejected and the lost, and welcome them into your hearts and homes.

Alleluia, alleluia, alleluia.

A reading from the Gospel according to Matthew/Mark/Luke
Alleluia, alleluia, alleluia.

A *Matthew 18.21–35*
B *Mark 8.27–38*
C *Luke 15.1–10*

Give glory to the living God.
Alleluia, alleluia, alleluia.
Unfold the Living Word for us today.

THE SUNDAY BETWEEN 11 AND 17 SEPTEMBER

Collects

Year A

Living Presence,
   vulnerable in love,
      never refusing to forgive those who have done great harm,
      never sealing yourself off from those who are in pain,
channel our anger,
   deepen our compassion,
      and open our hearts,
that we may be true to your name,
   however costly the way may prove to be.
We pray this after the pattern of Jesus
   and in the power of the Spirit.

Year B

Living Presence, turning us upside down,
   revealed to us in your chosen and anointed One,
   not as a warrior king but as a rejected outcast,
teach us to question the power we have,
   give us a generous heart to share it,
   and enable us, when the time is right,
      to become powerless, for love's sake.
We pray this after the pattern of Jesus
   and in the power of the Spirit.

Year C

Living Presence, prophetic and subversive,
   exalting those we think inferior to ourselves,
   toppling the pride of the wealthy and powerful,
give us grace to welcome those
   whose company risks our reputations,

THE SUNDAY BETWEEN 11 AND 17 SEPTEMBER

that we may find in their eyes and hands
>   the gifts of wisdom and love.
We pray this after the pattern of Jesus
>   and in the power of the Spirit.

4

Living Presence,
>   whose love embraces all the powers of creation,
>   and in whose company we need never be afraid,
give us steadiness and courage and skill
>   to strive with the energies
>   you have revealed in our discoveries,
that the wise use of heat and light, of atom and laser,
>   may enable the earth and its peoples
>   to flourish and prosper.
We pray this in the flow of the Spirit,
>   and after the pattern of Jesus,
>   true image of you, our Creator.

5

Living Presence of mystery and wonder,
>   moving the sun and the moon and the stars,
weave the patterns of glory
>   to the bounds of the universe,
>   even within the cells of our being.
We pray this in the energy of the Spirit,
>   and after the pattern of Jesus,
>   true image of you, our Creator.

THE SUNDAY BETWEEN 11 AND 17 SEPTEMBER

6

Living Presence of creative power,
   terrifying in intensity,
      in the chaos of the storm
      and in the tumult of our desires,
help us to understand the power of the atom
      and the fury of our hearts,
that the energies of the universe
   and the passions of our bodies
may be harnessed to serve the purposes of love,
   in the Spirit of Jesus,
     powerful in word and deed.

The Sunday between 18 and 24 September

Kyries

We have wasted too much time.

We have indulged ourselves in what is worthless.

We have accumulated junk that we do not need.

Response/Canticle/Hymn/Reflection

The Way of Love: 4 Love your enemies

Let us neither condemn nor destroy our enemies.
**Let us keep in 'contact' with them
even when we cannot keep 'in touch'.**
Let us strive powerfully with them, shoulder to shoulder,
until we see each other face to face.
Let us be angry,
but with compassion, not with hatred.
Let us not yield to fury,
nor to the resentment that leads to bitterness.
Let us be strongly and persuasively gentle –
with others and with ourselves.
Where there is ice in our hearts,
let it be melted by goodwill.

THE SUNDAY BETWEEN 18 AND 24 SEPTEMBER

Let us not meet oppression with violation –
we have all been too much hurt.
Our enemies are human beings much like ourselves:
let us not picture them as subhuman,
nor dismiss them with prejudice and insult.
Let us keep a sense of proportion –
and a sense of humour.
With an expanding heart
let us love our enemies.

Gospel Acclamation

Alleluia, alleluia, alleluia.
Alleluia, alleluia, alleluia.

A Give thanks to the God who is unfailingly generous.
B Whoever wants to lead must first learn what it is be nobody at all.
C Be faithful in small things. You cannot serve God and wealth.

Alleluia, alleluia, alleluia.

A reading from the Gospel according to Matthew/Mark/Luke
Alleluia, alleluia, alleluia.

A *Matthew 20.1–16*
B *Mark 9.30–37*
C *Luke 16.1–13*

Give glory to the living God.
Alleluia, alleluia, alleluia.
Unfold the Living Word for us today.

THE SUNDAY BETWEEN 18 AND 24 SEPTEMBER

Collects

Year A

Living Presence, unfailingly generous,
   making no distinctions of wealth or of ability,
root out from us the spirit of envy and greed,
and transform our bitterness
   into an open-hearted welcome
     of those we are tempted to despise.
We pray this after the pattern of Jesus
   and in the power of the Spirit.

Year B

Disturber of our false peace and uneasy truce,
   revealing to us that those who are powerless
     to make decisions that affect their lives
       are at the very centre of your domain,
humble us that we may see and hear
   those whom we usually ignore,
and learn from them how to be close to your heart,
   and to follow their example in our lives.
We pray this after the pattern of Jesus
   and in the power of the Spirit.

Year C

Living Presence of simplicity,
   showing us that we can be fully human
     yet possess nothing,
prune us of the securities
   with which we surround ourselves,
give us the folly of the Gospel
   which errs on the side of generosity,
and encourage us to give more than we receive.
We pray this after the pattern of Jesus
   and in the power of the Spirit.

THE SUNDAY BETWEEN 18 AND 24 SEPTEMBER

4

Living Presence, continually creating,
   celebrating with us
      a new unfolding of the universe this day,
   in us, in everything around us,
      and in the furthest star,
quieten our restless hearts and minds
   that we may listen to the silence,
      deepening as we hear
         the whispering of our breath,
         the hum of engines,
         the cries of birds,
that we may grow in wonder, awe, and adoration.
We pray this after the pattern of Jesus
   and in the power of the Spirit.

5

Living Presence of boundless energy,
   for ever creating and restoring,
forgive our rape of the earth,
   our greed and envy,
and give us your compassionate anger,
that we may live and work in harmony with you
   for the healing of the body of this planet,
      gasping for air,
      sores weeping on its skin,
that we may become people of one earth,
   its body and ours no longer violated,
      but nurtured and tended towards a flourishing
      we thought we would never see.
We pray this after the pattern of Jesus
   and in the power of the Spirit.

6

Creator Spirit,
>   whose script runs through the universe,
>   alive in each and every cell of our being,
> surge through us
>   with the thunder of the pounding waves,
> breathe through us
>   with the whisper of the evening breeze,
> dance through us
>   with the leaping flames of the sun,
> and ripple through us
>   with the merriment of the mountain stream,
> as it is with the power and spirit of Jesus,
>   in whom we pray.

The Sunday between 25 September and 1 October

Kyries

We have polluted the oceans with waste and have not paid to make them clean.

We have overfished the oceans and have not replenished them.

We have taken for granted those who risk their lives at sea on our behalf.

Response/Canticle/Hymn/Reflection

The Way of Love: 5 Rooted in love

According to the riches of God's glory
may we be strengthened with power
through the Spirit in our inner being,
and may Christ dwell in our hearts through faith,
that being rooted and grounded in love
**we may have power to comprehend with all the saints
the breadth and length and height and depth of love,**
and to know the love of Christ which passes knowledge,
**that we may be filled with the abundant life that is the gift of
   God alone.**

THE SUNDAY BETWEEN 25 SEPTEMBER AND 1 OCTOBER

Gospel Acclamation

Alleluia, alleluia, alleluia.
Alleluia, alleluia, alleluia.

- A Be faithful in small things. You cannot serve God and wealth.
- B Whoever is not against us is for us.
- C If you have not heard the prophets, what is your faith in resurrection worth?

Alleluia, alleluia, alleluia.

A reading from the Gospel according to Matthew/Mark/Luke
Alleluia, alleluia, alleluia.

- A *Matthew 21.23–32*
- B *Mark 9.38–50*
- C *Luke 16.19–31*

Give glory to the living God.
Alleluia, alleluia, alleluia.
Unfold the Living Word for us today.

Collects

Year A

Living Presence of searing truth,
   sending us prophets
     whose message makes us squirm,
melt the hardness of our hearts,
   and set our feet once more on the path of justice,
that we may take our part
   in the making right of relationships gone awry.
We pray this after the pattern of Jesus
   and in the power of the Spirit.

THE SUNDAY BETWEEN 25 SEPTEMBER AND 1 OCTOBER

Year B

Living Presence of clear sight and refining fire,
   bringing laser and scalpel to our pride and greed,
purge us of feeling superior
   to those who do not believe,
   or who believe in ways different from our own,
and let them shame us to repentance
   by their generous and humble deeds.
We pray this after the pattern of Jesus
   and in the power of the Spirit.

Year C

Living Presence of justice,
   mending relationships that have been torn apart,
keep us from too complacent a faith,
   lest we load on to others
     what we should rightly bear ourselves,
   and lest we forget the cost of making all things well.
We pray this after the pattern of Jesus
   and in the power of the Spirit.

4

Living Presence, bounteous and generous,
   showering us with gifts
     we so often take for granted,
enable us so to appreciate the gift of the harvest
   that we may know it as a pledge
     of abundant life,
   and that we may thank you
     as the source and goal of all that is good.
We pray this after the pattern of Jesus
   and in the power of the Spirit.

THE SUNDAY BETWEEN 25 SEPTEMBER AND 1 OCTOBER

5

Living Presence of wisdom and justice,
    hearing the cry of our prayer
    and knowing the reality of our politics,
renew in all of us a thirst for justice,
that we may cherish the earth and the oceans,
    teaching one another the wisdom of restraint,
    and nurturing a deep desire for the common good.
We pray this after the pattern of Jesus
    and in the power of the Spirit.

6

Living Presence beyond our conceiving and imagining,
    giving us the grace of patience and endurance,
    of contemplation and discernment,
may we hold in your presence and to your heart
    all that is intractable and unresolved
        in the life of this planet and its peoples,
        and in our own lives also,
that the time may come
    when the spirit of gratitude spreads over all things,
    and for all that has been
        we shall in truth give our thanks,
    and to all that is coming to be
        we shall indeed sing our Yes.
We pray this after the pattern of Jesus
    and in the power of the Spirit.

The Sunday between 2 and 8 October

Kyries

We have eroded the soil of the earth.

We have polluted the air of the skies.

We have poisoned the water of the oceans.

Response/Canticle/Hymn/Reflection

The paradoxes of faith

The greatest of treasures
with no worldly value
are as free as the air.
**The only monarchs
in God's own domain
are butterflies.**

If Christ is not risen
we are not risen:
**if we are not risen
Christ is not risen.**

Those who are not for us
are against us.
**Those who are not against us
are for us.**

THE SUNDAY BETWEEN 2 AND 8 OCTOBER

If you save your life
you will lose it.
**If you lose your life
you will save it.**

Powerful is the King of kings
and Lord of lords.
**Powerless is the Fool of fools,
the Clown of clowns.**

The greatest of treasures
with no worldly value
are as free as the air.
**The only monarchs
in God's own domain
are butterflies.**

Gospel Acclamation

Alleluia, alleluia, alleluia.
Alleluia, alleluia, alleluia.

A The stone which the builder rejected has become the cornerstone.
B Recognize the living Christ in each and every one you meet.
C Deepen your trust in the power of God.

Alleluia, alleluia, alleluia.

A reading from the Gospel according to Matthew/Mark/Luke
Alleluia, alleluia, alleluia.

A *Matthew 21.33–46*
B *Mark 10.2–16*
C *Luke 17.5–10*

Give glory to the living God.
Alleluia, alleluia, alleluia.
Unfold the Living Word for us today.

Collects

Year A

Source of all life,
   giving us people and places to care for,
prune us when need be,
   and keep us maturing in faithfulness,
that we may bear fruit to your glory,
   and to the common good of humankind.
We pray this after the pattern of Jesus
   and in the power of the Spirit.

Year B

Living Presence of love,
   revealed to us as justice in public
   and as intimacy in private,
take from us all thoughts
   of being superior or inferior to others,
and show us how to care for those close to us
   when they are more vulnerable than we are,
discerning always with your eyes
   that each of us is of infinite worth.
We pray this after the pattern of Jesus
   and in the power of the Spirit.

Year C

Faithful Presence,
   constant and loyal in your purposes,
      however obscure they may seem,

THE SUNDAY BETWEEN 2 AND 8 OCTOBER

increase our trust in you,
    and keep us steady in our obedience to your will,
that your life within us
    may move us to do greater things
        than we have ever imagined.
We pray this after the pattern of Jesus
    and in the power of the Spirit.

4

Wounded, glorified Healer, shining with scars,
    taking to yourself our outraged and wounded hearts,
console our grief, melt our fear,
    lift the burden of our shame,
that we may restrain our desire for revenge,
    and channel the fierce energies of our anger
        in the service of justice and a world become whole.
We pray this after the pattern of Jesus
    and in the power of the Spirit.

5

Living Presence of wisdom,
    guiding those who ask
        with your Spirit of true counsel,
encourage those with power
    to discern the course that is just,
    to lay aside all pride of wealth and status,
    and to sacrifice themselves for the common good,
        not only of their own land,
        but also of the whole earth.
We pray this after the pattern of Jesus
    and in the power of the Spirit.

6

Living Presence,
> steadying us in the midst of our storms,

gently move within us,
> even in the doubtings of our minds,
> the fickleness of our wills,
> and the betrayals of our hearts,

that we may be startled afresh,
> our breath taken away,
> and our trust renewed.

We pray this after the pattern of Jesus
> and in the power of the Spirit.

The Sunday between 9 and 15 October

Kyries

We have taken from the soil,
and we have not replenished the earth.

We have polluted the water,
and we have not paid enough for its cleansing.

We have poisoned the air,
and we have postponed tough decisions.

Response/Canticle/Hymn/Reflection

A World Divinely Human – 'In Christ'

Mysterious presence ... **dazzling darkness** ...
glory beyond glory ... **light within light** ... .
greater than all ... **hidden in all** ...
way beyond words ... **silence deeper than silence** ...
empty ... **full** ...
absent ... **present** ...
narrow point ... **unending space** ...
no-thing ... **every-thing** ...
no-body ... **every-body** ...

THE SUNDAY BETWEEN 9 AND 15 OCTOBER

air in which all bodies breathe ...
ocean in which all waves move ...
underground in which all things root their being ...
filling us to overflowing ...
with awesome wonder ...
with powerful love ...
with deep thankfulness ...
with lingering adoration ...
evolving ... **emerging** ...
taking shape ... **flesh and blood** ...
human being ... **fully alive** ...
wise ... discerning ... truthful ...
just ... kind ... **patient** ...
giving life ... bearing pain ... **making love** ...
dissolving evil ... transfiguring suffering ...
swallowing death ...
threshold ... gateway ... **pioneer** ...
slave ... fool ... **lamb** ...
childlike ... foolish ... **homeless** ...
laying aside worldly power ... refusing all titles ...
washing feet ...
inspiring us ... **for intimacy and trust** ...
energizing us ... **for justice and compassion** ...
nourishing one another ...
forgiving one another ...
liberating one another ...
healing one another ...
encouraging one another ...
strengthening one another ...
enfolding ... enlivening ... **empowering** ...
everywhere ... **always** ...
here ... now ...
yes ... **so be it.**

THE SUNDAY BETWEEN 9 AND 15 OCTOBER

Gospel Acclamation

Alleluia, alleluia, alleluia.
Alleluia, alleluia, alleluia.

A   Go into the streets and invite everyone to the banquet.
B   The word of God is living and active, judging the thoughts and intentions of the heart.
C   Be grateful, to seventy times seven.

Alleluia, alleluia, alleluia.

A reading from the Gospel according to Matthew/Mark/Luke
Alleluia, alleluia, alleluia.

A   *Matthew 22.1–14*
B   *Mark 10.17–31*
C   *Luke 17.11–19*

Give glory to the living God.
Alleluia, alleluia, alleluia.
Unfold the Living Word for us today.

Collects

Year A

Hospitable Presence,
   inviting us to your table when we least expect it,
halt our excuses from the pressure of other concerns,
   and humble us to wear the garment
      that hides all signs of wealth and status;
turn us around from slinking away
   from feelings of unworthiness and shame,
   and warm us with the garment
      that preserves our dignity;

THE SUNDAY BETWEEN 9 AND 15 OCTOBER

so may we meet others as fellow guests
>who, with gratitude, delight in one another as equals
>in the presence of their host.

We pray this after the pattern of Jesus
>and in the power of the Spirit.

Year B

Living Presence of stern and clear love,
>facing us with the needle's eye,

slim us down, prune our possessions,
>dismantle the walls of our defences,

that we may find courage
>to go through the narrow gate
>>leading to the wide open country of your freedom,

and so give us a glimpse
>of what your salvation means.

We pray this after the pattern of Jesus
>and in the power of the Spirit.

Year C

Living Presence of compassion and healing,
>touching our lives by human skills
>and by means as yet unknown to us,

give us the spirit of gratitude
>for our recoveries of health,
>and for the reconciliations
>>that follow the swallowing of our pride,

that we may be ready to be thankful
>even in the midst of troubles
>>that do not go away,

for your strangest gifts to us
>are beyond anything we could ever imagine.

We pray this after the pattern of Jesus
>and in the power of the Spirit.

THE SUNDAY BETWEEN 9 AND 15 OCTOBER

4

Living Presence, just, true, and generous,
   embracing us despite our imperfections,
   relaxing us into the truth
     that we need not strive to be perfect,
   taking from us our overbearing demands on others,
give us your Spirit that leaves no room for hatred or envy,
that we may no longer howl with glee
   when those in public life let us down.
We pray this after the pattern of Jesus
   and in the power of the Spirit.

5

Living Presence of power and mercy,
   revealing to us
     that anger and compassion join together
       in bringing justice and healing in the world,
keep our anger within bounds
   so that it does not destroy,
and keep our caring truthful,
   so that we do not allow ourselves to be destroyed.
We pray this after the pattern of Jesus
   and in the power of the Spirit.

6

Living Presence, powerfully unlike all worldly power,
   with infinite compassion and grace
     yearning to rescue us from all that enslaves us,
call us out of our imprisonments,
   however comfortable they have come to be,
and lead us to the wide open spaces
   of your bracing freedom.
We pray this after the pattern of Jesus
   and in the power of the Spirit.

The Sunday between 16 and 22 October

Kyries

We have wounded your body,
the good earth from which our bodies come.

We have wounded the bodies of others,
and not taken enough care of them.

We have wounded our own bodies,
and have not cherished them.

Response/Canticle/Hymn/Reflection

Trusting (An unfolding of part of Isaiah 43.1–4)

You have created us
and you continue to shape us ...
You have rescued us
and you are liberating us ...
You have brought us a measure of healing,
and you are restoring us ...
You call us by name,
and we belong to you ...
You are present with us on our journey,
steady companion at our side ...

THE SUNDAY BETWEEN 16 AND 22 OCTOBER

When we wade through turbulent waves,
the water will not drown us ...
When we struggle against gusts and squalls,
the wind will not cast us down ...
When we flinch through flames,
the fire will not consume us ...
For you are the Living One,
loving us beyond compare,
as the most precious jewels in your sight,
honouring us beyond deserving ...
Again and again you reassure us:
Do not be afraid ...

Gospel Acclamation

Alleluia, alleluia, alleluia.
Alleluia, alleluia, alleluia.

A   God first! God first!
B   What do you want Christ to do for you?
C   Embody Christ's passion for justice.

Alleluia, alleluia, alleluia.

A reading from the Gospel according to Matthew/Mark/Luke
Alleluia, alleluia, alleluia.

A   *Matthew 22.15–22*
B   *Mark 10.35–45*
C   *Luke 18.1–8*

Give glory to the living God.
Alleluia, alleluia, alleluia.
Unfold the Living Word for us today.

THE SUNDAY BETWEEN 16 AND 22 OCTOBER

Collects

Year A

Living Presence of true well-being,
   showing us how greed for money
   is the root of all evil,
deepen our awareness of how wealth can
   oppress and defraud the poor
   and harden the hearts of the rich,
that we may gird ourselves with courage
   to enable your commonwealth
     to be glimpsed among us,
   as we share our possessions and open our hearts.
We pray this after the pattern of Jesus
   and in the power of the Spirit.

Year B

Living Presence of a wisdom far beyond our own,
   facing us with challenges we would rather avoid,
   yet seeking to bring harmony to our disordered lives,
give us courage to pay the price of true love,
so that you may bring us to our hearts' true desire,
   our deepest yearnings and longings at last fulfilled.
We pray this after the pattern of Jesus
   and in the power of the Spirit.

Year C

Living Presence of justice,
   painstakingly repairing relationships torn apart,
inspire us with passion and endurance
   to embody your ways on earth,
that oppression and injustice may vanish from our lives.
We pray this after the pattern of Jesus
   and in the power of the Spirit.

THE SUNDAY BETWEEN 16 AND 22 OCTOBER

4

Faithful Creator,
  ever striving with your creation,
    with nature,
    with your people,
    with the One who embodied your will,
  bringing new and unexpected life
    out of despair and death,
work still in these our days
  that we may sing a new song to your glory.
We pray this after the pattern of Jesus
  and in the power of the Spirit.

5

Living Presence of the promises that stand for ever,
  tearing us apart when we see them unfulfilled,
  shrivelling us through perplexity and doubt,
  extinguishing the flickering lights of reassurance,
keep us faithful through our winter,
that the slender thread of trust may hold.
We pray this after the pattern of Jesus
  and in the power of the Spirit.

6

Rescuer and Redeemer,
  presence in the midst of storm and tempest,
be with us in the darker places of faith's journey,
  and help us discern our freedom
    in choosing what is difficult as if it were easy,
for then we shall have faith indeed,
  and even at the bleakest times we shall praise.
We pray this after the pattern of Jesus
  and in the power of the Spirit.

The Sunday between 23 and 29 October

Kyries

We have been hurt, and we have hurt others.

We have been harmed, and we have harmed others.

We have been wounded, and we have wounded others.

Response/Canticle/Hymn/Reflection

Trusting (inspired by Charles de Foucauld)

AbbaAmma, Beloved Friend,
I give myself into your hands ...
In your *love* for me,
weave your will into the fabric of my life ...
Whatever that may bring,
and wherever that may lead,
give me the courage to be steadfast
give me the grace to be thankful ...
Prepare me to be ready for all,
to accept everything that shall come ...
As in all life in this evolving universe,
drawing me into a future unknown,

THE SUNDAY BETWEEN 23 AND 29 OCTOBER

let only your will be done in me,
and I will ask nothing else ...
Into your hands I commend the whole of my life.
for I love you, Loving Presence in my heart ...
Steady my will to lay aside my surface self
and to let my deep self be the centre of my being ...
For you are faithfully creating me,
giving me life, bearing my pain, making love with me ...
I trust you without reserve,
AbbaAmma, Beloved Friend ...

Gospel Acclamation

Alleluia, alleluia, alleluia.
Alleluia, alleluia, alleluia.

A Above all else, love God with the whole of your being.
B Jesus asked, What do you want me to do for you?
C Those who humble themselves will be exalted.

Alleluia, alleluia, alleluia.

A reading from the Gospel according to Matthew/Mark/Luke
Alleluia, alleluia, alleluia.

A Matthew 22.34–46
B Mark 10.46–52
C Luke 18.9–14

Give glory to the living God.
Alleluia, alleluia, alleluia.
Unfold the Living Word for us today.

THE SUNDAY BETWEEN 23 AND 29 OCTOBER

Collects

Year A

Loving Presence,
   giving us grace to respond to your invitation
   to follow your way,
enable us
   to love one another as you have loved us,
   to love our neighbours as ourselves,
   to love even our enemies,
and
   to love you with all our heart and mind and strength,
   and ever to abide in your love.
We pray this after the pattern of Jesus
   and in the power of the Spirit.

Year B

Passionate Presence,
   revealing to us the power of determined desire
   in the blind man who cried out more earnestly
     the second time,
   and who leapt to his feet when he was called,
give us the honesty and clarity
   to become aware of our own deepest desire,
and the single-minded energy
   to pursue it in our reaching out to you.
We pray this after the pattern of Jesus
   and in the power of the Spirit.

Year C

Living Presence of overflowing generosity
    and unbounded love,
   looking not at surface things
     but deep into the human heart,

THE SUNDAY BETWEEN 23 AND 29 OCTOBER

increase our gratitude for your gifts,
that we may not be distracted by glamour and glitter,
> but steadfastly love mercy,
> act with kindness,
> and walk humbly with you.
We pray this after the pattern of Jesus
> and in the power of the Spirit.

4

Hidden Presence,
> hard to believe in,
> testing our faith to prove its worth,
bring us through the dark nights
> of our doubts and fears and emptiness,
that we may rejoice in the dawn
> and join our ancestors in dancing your praise.
We pray this after the pattern of Jesus
> and in the power of the Spirit.

5

Living Presence,
> the same yesterday, today, and for ever,
whose presence we have lost
> in a bleak despairing time,
focus our minds and hearts
> on those memories of grace
>> that surprised us and lightened our burden,
so that faith may be kept alive,
> hope may be rekindled,
>> and gratitude whispered,
>>> even in the darkest night.
We pray this after the pattern of Jesus
> and in the power of the Spirit.

THE SUNDAY BETWEEN 23 AND 29 OCTOBER

6

Eternal Presence,
   embracing time in creation,
     giving us its measure for our fleeting years,
       which pass so quickly as to dent our pride,
may we neither rely on our achievements
   nor be downcast at our failures,
and keep us but faithful to your love,
   and dependent on your grace alone.
We ask this in the Spirit of the One
   who died a human failure,
     and died so young.

The Fourth Sunday before Advent, between 30 October and 5 November

Kyries

We have refused to enter our own dark places
and let the light of the saints shine on them.

We have not let ourselves be still in your presence
and let the light of Christ transform our faces.

We have not believed that you wish to make us holy,
nor that we should even desire to be transformed.

Or:

We have not consciously sent our love
   to those who have died before us.

We have not asked them to send us their love and their light,
radiant with the divine in them.

We have not been angry at how unfair it is
   that too many lives are so brief and wracked with pain.

THE FOURTH SUNDAY BEFORE ADVENT

Response/Canticle/Hymn/Reflection

Beloved Jesus, embodier of God,
vulnerable, wounded, pinioned to death,
your power came to full strength in weakness,
dissolving evil, transforming pain, swallowing death.
Your victory will be shared by your followers,
called and chosen and faithful. Alleluia!

These are the words of the First and the Last,
who was dead and came to life again:

To the one who is victorious
I shall give the right to eat from the Tree of Life
that stands in the garden of God. Alleluia!
Be faithful to death,
and I shall give you the crown of life. Alleluia!

To the one who is victorious
I shall give some of the hidden manna,
and I shall give also a white stone. Alleluia!
And on the stone will be written a new name,
known only to the one who receives it. Alleluia!

To the one who is victorious,
who perseveres in doing my will to the end,
I shall give authority among the nations. Alleluia!
It is the same authority that I received from the Eternal,
illuminated by the gift of the star of dawn. Alleluia!

The one who is victorious
will be made a pillar in the temple of God
and will never leave it. Alleluia!
Upon that pillar I shall write the name of my God
and the name of the city of my God,
and my own new name. Alleluia!

THE FOURTH SUNDAY BEFORE ADVENT

To the one who is victorious
I shall give a place in my company,
as I myself was victorious. Alleluia!
We shall dwell in the presence of the Eternal. Alleluia!

These are the words of the Amen,
the faithful and true witness.

Beloved Jesus, embodier of God,
vulnerable, wounded, pinioned to death,
your power came to full strength in weakness,
dissolving evil, transforming pain, swallowing death.
Your victory will be shared by your followers,
called and chosen and faithful. Alleluia!

Gospel Acclamation

Alleluia, alleluia, alleluia.
Alleluia, alleluia, alleluia.

- A Not one stone here shall be left upon another.
- B The time is fulfilled: the kingdom of God is near.
  Love is the fulfilling of the law.
- C Welcome Christ as your guest in heart and home.

Alleluia, alleluia, alleluia.

A reading from the Gospel according to Matthew/Mark/Luke
Alleluia, alleluia, alleluia.

- A *Matthew 24.1–14*
- B *Mark 12.28–34*
- C *Luke 19.1–10*

Give glory to the living God.
Alleluia, alleluia, alleluia.
Unfold the Living Word for us today.

THE FOURTH SUNDAY BEFORE ADVENT

Collects

Year A

Living Presence, steady as a rock,
  placing before us stones to raise
    and stones to stumble over,
help us to discern when to build
  and when to dismantle,
knowing that nothing that we do
  can last for ever,
and that the Christ is the only cornerstone we need.
We pray this after the pattern of Jesus
  and in the power of the Spirit.

Year B

Living Presence of love,
  revealing to human beings
    your nature and your name,
empower us to fulfil your commandments
  to love you,
    and to love our neighbours as ourselves,
so that we may give, whatever the cost,
  to enable the well-being of those
    with whom we have to do,
  even and especially our enemies.
We pray this after the pattern of Jesus
  and in the power of the Spirit.

THE FOURTH SUNDAY BEFORE ADVENT

Year C

Living Presence, welcoming and generous,
   knowing that we human beings
      grow in love for one another
      in exchanges of mercy and grace,
give us the discernment and the humility
   to ask a favour from others,
that by respecting their dignity
   and depending upon them,
we may open both our heart and theirs
   to the spirit of friendship.
We pray this after the pattern of Jesus
   and in the power of the Spirit.

Collects for weekdays between between 30 October and 14 November, excluding All Saints' Day, All Souls' Day, Armistice Day

1

Holy Presence,
   whose saints we celebrate at this time,
give us wisdom to discern
   that holiness is not a virtue to strive for
   but a gift to prepare for,
give us the clarity to perceive such holiness in others,
and give us the sanity never to claim it for ourselves.
We pray this after the pattern of Jesus
   and in the power of the Spirit.

2

Living Presence,
   whose love is so powerful
     that it dissolves the chains of death,
liberate us from all that holds us down,
that we may come out into the light,
   and run free in the wind,
   and know the lasting joy of your saints.
We pray this after the pattern of Jesus
   and in the power of the Spirit.

3

Living Presence of impossible holiness,
　　shaking us to the very foundations of our being,
　　giving us new life
　　　　in the midst of disgrace and despair,
　　　　when every door seems shut against us,
　　showering us with the grace to love those
　　　　whose eyes would destroy us,
encourage us with the example of your saints,
　　that we in turn may join the great cloud of witnesses,
　　and shine with eyes of compassion and glory.
We pray this after the pattern of Jesus
　　and in the power of the Spirit.

4

Living Presence to Abraham, to Isaac and to Jacob,
　　the God not of the dead but of the living,
lead us all through life and death,
　　through flow and ebb, through light and dark,
that we may never lose a quiet conviction
　　that your love binds us all together,
　　and that nothing can separate us from your presence.
We pray this after the pattern of Jesus
　　and in the power of the Spirit.

5

Living Presence,
　　faithful to your call and trustworthy in your promises,
sanctify those whom we love who have died before us,
bless them richly,
　　that they may grow in grace, and make love,
　　that they may keep us in loving mind, and guide us,
　　that they may hold us close in your presence,
　　　　and pray with us.
We ask this in and through Jesus Christ,
　　who broke the barrier of death and is alive for ever.

6

Protector and deliverer of humankind,
   whose heart yearns for us to do your will
   and follow your way,
hear our desperate cries,
   set us free from violence,
   relieve the agony of oppression,
   melt the ice of our fears,
from the places of your silence
   give us courage to do your will,
and give us the steadfastness step by step
     to follow your way.
We pray this after the pattern of Jesus
   and in the power of the Spirit.

7

Living Presence,
   faithful to your covenant with the earth,
steady our hearts and wills
   in times of great turbulence,
that we may fulfil your purpose for us
   as heralds and enablers
     of your just and lasting peace.
We pray this after the pattern of Jesus
   and in the power of the Spirit.

8

Living Presence of compassion and justice,
   empowering Jesus to cure disease
     by word and touch,
   and to heal divisions
     by embracing the outcast and stigmatized,

take from us all prejudice and fear,
    and inspire us with courage and an open heart
        to enjoy the company of the despised and rejected,
that together we may know that we belong in your domain.
We pray this in the Spirit of the universal Christ,
    incarnate and glorified,
        humanity alive in you for ever.

9

Loving Presence,
    resisting evil by absorbing and dissolving it,
take from us all desire to harm,
    and all thirst for vengeance,
wean us from our addiction to violence,
open our eyes
    that we may see that those who trouble us
        are our equals in dignity and worth,
and strengthen our wills to love them without reserve.
We pray this in the Spirit of the universal Christ,
    incarnate and glorified,
        humanity alive in you for ever.

10

Living Presence of beauty and bounty,
    whose gifts we have desecrated,
    and whose renewal we have presumed,
give us penitent hearts
    and the will to cherish the earth,
that we may know you again
    as a redeeming and restoring presence,
        bringing good from our wastes and sorrows.
We pray this after the pattern of Jesus
    and in the power of the Spirit.

COLLECTS FOR WEEKDAYS 30 OCTOBER–14 NOVEMBER

11

Living Presence of marvel and wonder,
   open our eyes
      beyond the puzzling reflections in a mirror,
      beyond the brutal images of violence,
      beyond the fading of the years,
that we may see true and clear
   the wide open spaces of promised freedom,
that we may glimpse the communion of saints
   and brush the wings of angels,
that we may recognize for a moment
   the glory of the universe,
      where darkness and doubt dissolve,
      where the gash of the wound shines,
      where death and destruction vanish for ever.
We pray this after the pattern of Jesus
   and in the power of the Spirit.

12

Living Presence to Abraham and Sarah,
   bringing them and us more abundantly alive,
and, in Jesus, bringing out of the gloom
   of the place of the departed
   all our ancestors of faith,
renew our hope in the glory that shall be,
   when we and all whom we remember
   shall be united in wonder and the song of rejoicing.
We pray this after the pattern of Jesus
   and in the power of the Spirit.

All Saints' Day

Years A, B, C

Living Presence,
   whose fierce eye is never without gentleness,
   and whose saints calmed the fiercest of the creatures,
melt the fear that makes us defensive,
and fill us with such serenity
   that nothing will be able to disturb us
     in the deep centre of our being,
so that we may be adamant
   in protecting the vulnerable,
   and gentle with their wounds.
So make us and keep us holy,
   in the glorious communion of your saints.
We pray this after the pattern of Jesus
   and in the power of the Spirit.

All Souls' Day

Years A, B, C

Living One, in whose embrace all creatures live,
   in whatever world or condition they may be,
as we remember in your presence
   those we have known and loved,
   whose names and needs and dwelling places
     are known to you ... [NN]
and as we give you thanks for them,
   loving them for all that they have meant to us,
   and loving them as they are
     in your inexhaustible love,
may this our prayer minister to their peace,
   and to their growth in grace.
We pray this in and through Jesus Christ,
   who broke the barrier of death and is alive for ever.

Remembrance

Years A, B, C

Living Presence of wisdom and compassion,
 whose will is fiery for justice,
guide those who bear office in public life,
that they may use their power for the common good,
 in village, town, and city,
 in this and every land,
that your commonwealth of justice and peace
 may indeed come on earth.
We pray this after the pattern of Jesus
 and in the power of the Spirit.

All Saints' Day
Years A, B, C

Kyries

We have refused to enter our own dark places
and let the light of the saints shine on them.

We have not let ourselves be still in your presence
and let the light of Christ transform our faces.

We have not believed that you wish to make us holy,
nor that we should even desire to be transformed.

Response/Canticle/Hymn/Reflection

Beloved Jesus, embodier of God,
vulnerable, wounded, pinioned to death,
your power came to full strength in weakness,
dissolving evil, transforming pain, swallowing death.
Your victory will be shared by your followers,
called and chosen and faithful. Alleluia!

These are the words of the First and the Last,
who was dead and came to life again:

To the one who is victorious
I shall give the right to eat from the Tree of Life

ALL SAINTS' DAY

that stands in the garden of God. Alleluia!
**Be faithful to death,
and I shall give you the crown of life. Alleluia!**

To the one who is victorious
I shall give some of the hidden manna,
and I shall give also a white stone. Alleluia!
**And on the stone will be written a new name,
known only to the one who receives it. Alleluia!**

To the one who is victorious,
who perseveres in doing my will to the end,
I shall give authority among the nations. Alleluia!
**It is the same authority that I received from the Eternal,
illuminated by the gift of the star of dawn. Alleluia!**

The one who is victorious
will be made a pillar in the temple of God
and will never leave it. Alleluia!
**Upon that pillar I shall write the name of my God
and the name of the city of my God,
and my own new name. Alleluia!**

To the one who is victorious
I shall give a place in my company,
as I myself was victorious. Alleluia!
We shall dwell in the presence of the Eternal. Alleluia!

These are the words of the Amen,
the faithful and true witness.

Beloved Jesus, embodier of God,
vulnerable, wounded, pinioned to death,
your power came to full strength in weakness,
dissolving evil, transforming pain, swallowing death.
Your victory will be shared by your followers,
called and chosen and faithful. Alleluia!

Gospel Acclamation

Alleluia, alleluia, alleluia.
Alleluia, alleluia, alleluia.

Blessed are the gentle:
the freedom of the citizens of the earth is theirs.

Alleluia, alleluia, alleluia.

A reading from the Gospel according to Matthew
Alleluia, alleluia, alleluia.

Matthew 5.1–12

Give glory to the living God.
Alleluia, alleluia, alleluia.
Unfold the Living Word for us today.

Collect

Living Presence,
   whose fierce eye is never without gentleness,
   and whose saints calmed the fiercest of the creatures,
melt the fear that makes us defensive,
and fill us with such serenity
   that nothing will be able to disturb us
     in the deep centre of our being,
so that we may be adamant
   in protecting the vulnerable,
   and gentle with their wounds.
So make us and keep us holy,
   in the glorious communion of your saints.
We pray this after the pattern of Jesus
   and in the power of the Spirit.

All Souls' Day
Years A, B, C

Kyries

We have not consciously sent our love
   to those who have died before us.

We have not asked them to send us their love and their light,
radiant with the divine in them.

We have not been angry at how unfair it is
   that too many lives are so brief and wracked with pain.

Response/Canticle/Hymn/Reflection

I saw in my mind's eye a vision:
a new realm, a new order, a new earth,
for the old had decayed and passed away.
Even the seas of chaos had been calmed.

And I saw the holy city, new Jerusalem,
coming out of the clouds of God's presence,
prepared as a bride and bridegroom
are adorned as gifts to each other.

And I heard the voice of the One who reigns:
Behold, I come to dwell among you, my people,
and you will live in my presence.

I shall wipe away every tear from your eyes,
and death will be no more,
neither will there be mourning,
nor crying, nor pain, any more.
The former things have passed away:
Behold, I make all things new.

Gospel Acclamation

Alleluia, alleluia, alleluia.
Alleluia, alleluia, alleluia.

Hear the voice of God's Beloved: Believe, and you shall live.

Alleluia, alleluia, alleluia.

A reading from the Gospel according to John
Alleluia, alleluia, alleluia.

John 5.19–25 or 6.37–40

Give glory to the living God.
Alleluia, alleluia, alleluia.
Unfold the Living Word for us today.

ALL SOULS' DAY

Collect

Living One, in whose embrace all creatures live,
   in whatever world or condition they may be,
as we remember in your presence
   those we have known and loved,
     whose names and needs and dwelling places
       are known to you ... [NN]
and as we give you thanks for them,
   loving them for all that they have meant to us,
   and loving them as they are in your inexhaustible love,
may this our prayer minister to their peace,
   and to their growth in grace.
We pray this in and through Jesus Christ,
   who broke the barrier of death and is alive for ever.

The Third Sunday before Advent
The Sunday between the 6 and 12 November

Kyries

We find it hard to endure and we give up too easily.

We are lulled into sleep and we forget to keep awake.

We sink into complacency and are no longer alert.

Response/Canticle/Hymn/Reflection

One

No affliction, no hardship
nothing can separate us from the love of God.
No hunger, no thirst, no cold, no fire,
nothing can separate us from the love of God.
No persecution, no danger, no sword,
nothing can separate us from the love of God.
No terror, no knife, no bomb,
nothing can separate us from the love of God.
No land mines, no guns, no disease,
nothing can separate us from the love of God.
No poison, no shock, no sudden death,
nothing can separate us from the love of God.

THE THIRD SUNDAY BEFORE ADVENT

There is nothing in death or in life,
nothing can separate us from the love of God.
No powers that be, no evil's grip,
nothing can separate us from the love of God.
In the world as it is or the world as it shall be,
nothing can separate us from the love of God.
There is nothing in the whole of creation,
nothing can separate us from the love of God.

You have embodied your love for us in Jesus:
in your Spirit we stammer our thanks.
We shall trust in your presence through all that is to come.
Nothing can separate us from your love.

Two

On a beach, reflecting on our dying

On this familiar strand
our feet we lightly place:
we build our castle towers and walls
but leave behind no trace.

Relentlessly the sea
uncovers graves and stones,
reclaiming what we thought was ours,
our cells, our flesh, our bones.

The pincers of the crab
attack us from the side:
they drag us helpless, down and down,
through surf and ebbing tide.

THE THIRD SUNDAY BEFORE ADVENT

Our journey to the west
cannot postpone the sea:
eternity soon swallows time,
land's end for you and me.

Our body's fibres part,
the thread of gold is drawn,
ourselves slimmed down for needle's eye,
yet into glory born(e).

Gospel Acclamation

Alleluia, alleluia, alleluia.
Alleluia, alleluia, alleluia.

A Keep awake: truth will dawn at a time you least expect.
B The time is fulfilled: the kingdom of God is near.
C In Christ shall all be made alive.

Alleluia, alleluia, alleluia.

A reading from the Gospel according to Matthew/Mark/Luke
Alleluia, alleluia, alleluia.

A *Matthew 25.1–13*
B *Mark 1.14–20*
C *Luke 20.27–38*

Give glory to the living God.
Alleluia, alleluia, alleluia.
Unfold the Living Word for us today.

THE THIRD SUNDAY BEFORE ADVENT

Collects

Year A

Living Presence, alert and alight,
   as the earth sleeps
   and the darkness lengthens,
keep us watchful and alert,
   so that we are not lulled into lethargy
   and miss even the smallest of your gifts,
     always unexpected,
     and always for our greater good.
We pray this after the pattern of Jesus
   in the power of the Spirit,
   and in the promise of glory.

Year B

Living Presence, always near,
   whose domain is already among us,
keep us alert as we go about our daily tasks,
   that we may be ready to respond
     to whatever next it is that you are calling us to do.
We pray this after the pattern of Jesus
   in the power of the Spirit,
   and in the promise of glory.

Year C

Living Presence of life and joy,
   undermining the grim pernickety mind
     that is consumed with being in the right,
dissolve our self-righteousness
   with the grace of laughter,
that together we may dance with delight,
   in the joy of resurrection life.

THE THIRD SUNDAY BEFORE ADVENT

We pray this after the pattern of Jesus
   in the power of the Spirit,
   and in the promise of glory.

4

Living Presence of wisdom,
   in solidarity with the burden bearers,
   patiently negotiating among those who are at war,
steady our nerves
   and strengthen our wills,
that we too may pursue the way of reconciliation,
   among our families
   and in our communities,
that we may taste your kingdom come
   in the ways of compassion and justice,
   restored, reconciled, and renewed.
We pray this after the pattern of Jesus
   in the power of the Spirit,
   and in the promise of glory.

For further weekday collects see Collects for Weekdays, 30 October–14 November.

The Second Sunday before Advent
The Sunday between the 13 and 19 November

Kyries

We have not put the voice of the voiceless first.

We have colluded with the structures of greed.

We have put money first, loving it too much.

Response/Canticle/Hymn/Reflection

The Kingdom of God

A lamb is seated on a throne:
Mysterious and strange are your ways,
turning us upside down.

A child is at the centre of God's domain.
Mysterious and strange are your ways,
turning us upside down.

A slave woman, a nameless nobody
washes our feet and shows us God.
Mysterious and strange are your ways,
turning us upside down.

THE SECOND SUNDAY BEFORE ADVENT

The man in the ditch left for dead
has to receive the love of his enemy.
**Mysterious and strange are your ways,
turning us upside down.**

A crucified outcast shows the extent of God's love.
**Mysterious and strange are your ways,
turning us upside down.**

A nameless soldier in the enemy's army
is awed by this Presence of God.
**Mysterious and strange are your ways,
turning us upside down.**

Gospel Acclamation

Alleluia, alleluia, alleluia.
Alleluia, alleluia, alleluia.

A   Be faithful in small things.
B   Do not be distracted by the words or deeds of the powerful.
C   Listen for the words of wisdom that cannot be extinguished.

Alleluia, alleluia, alleluia.

A reading from the Gospel according to Matthew/Mark/Luke
Alleluia, alleluia, alleluia.

A   *Matthew 25.14–30*
B   *Mark 13.1–8*
C   *Luke 21.5–19*

Give glory to the living God.
Alleluia, alleluia, alleluia.
Unfold the Living Word for us today.

THE SECOND SUNDAY BEFORE ADVENT

Collects

Year A

Gracious Presence,
  showering us with gifts
    and challenging us to use them
      to serve that which is greater than ourselves,
may we be humble enough
  to receive what you give for our delight,
and selfless enough
  to give of ourselves for others,
so that we and all whom we meet may flourish,
  and grow to maturity in you.
We pray this after the pattern of Jesus
  in the power of the Spirit,
  and in the promise of glory.

Year B

Living Presence to the silenced and the unnoticed,
  who, above all, are at home in your domain,
  whose narrow gate slims down
    the powerful and the wealthy,
open our eyes to the beauty
  of the vulnerable and the small,
and keep us from being seduced
  by great buildings and strong armies.
We pray this after the pattern of Jesus
  and in the power of the Spirit,
  and in the promise of glory.

Year C

Living Presence,
   awakening and disturbing us,
   whose challenge our surface selves resist,
teach us your wisdom
   and root it deep within our being,
so that, whenever we are opposed
   because we believe in your name,
the right words will rise unbidden to our lips.
We pray this after the pattern of Jesus
   in the power of the Spirit,
   and in the promise of glory.

4

Living Presence of unfailing hope
   ever present with us
      through the depths of our despair,
work in us the costly ways of peace,
   that in justice and with gentleness
      your will may be done on earth.
We pray this after the pattern of Jesus
   in the power of the Spirit,
   and in the promise of glory.

5

Living Presence,
   moving through the vastness of the universe,
     of which we are so small a part,
   swamping us with fear and despair,
     gripped by how insignificant we seem,
deepen our trust that the meaning of it all is love,
   beyond whose reach it is impossible to fall.
We pray this after the pattern of Jesus
   and in the power of the Spirit,
   and in the promise of glory.

6

Searching and luring Presence,
   seeking us out amid the immensities of the universe,
   calling us to be partners
     in the work of your creating,
give us hearts that respond
   and wills that are determined,
that we may not fail you,
   but take our part
     in the transforming of the earth to glory.
We pray this after the pattern of Jesus
   in the power of the Spirit,
   and in the promise of glory.

Christ the King –
The Sunday next before Advent
The Sunday between
20 and 26 November

Kyries

As nations,
    we are still too much afraid of one another.

As citizens,
    we collude with the making of instruments of mass
      destruction and threatening their use.

As individuals,
    we keep silent when we should speak out.

Response/Canticle/Hymn/Reflection

Based on the Lord's Prayer

(as unfolded by John Dominic Crossan in The Greatest Prayer*)*

You are the householder of the world,
you are the homemaker of the earth.
Your son and heir is Jesus,
whose joint heirs you call us to be.

THE SUNDAY NEXT BEFORE ADVENT

The deepest desire of your heart –
the hallowing of your name, your character –
is for us to take our part with him
in the coming of your commonwealth,
the fulfilment of your will for justice,
as in your heaven so on this earth:
Enough human food for today!
No human debt for tomorrow!
Human violence no more than memory,
human justice shaping the peace!
In no other way can your wisdom rule,
in no other way can the power of love reign.
In no other way can your glory be seen.
And so may it be, our heartfelt Amen.

Gospel Acclamation

Alleluia, alleluia, alleluia.
Alleluia, alleluia, alleluia.

A As you act towards the least in the eyes of the world, so act towards Christ.
B Are you a king?
C He saved others: he cannot save himself.

Alleluia, alleluia, alleluia.

A reading from the Gospel according to Matthew/John/Luke
Alleluia, alleluia, alleluia.

A *Matthew 25.31–46*
B *John 18.33–37*
C *Luke 3.33–43*

Give glory to the living God.
Alleluia, alleluia, alleluia.
Unfold the Living Word for us today.

THE SUNDAY NEXT BEFORE ADVENT

Collects

Year A

Living Presence in simple things,
   the strangest of monarchs,
   with no worldly power,
   both lamb and child,
alert us to your presence in
   the vulnerable and young,
   the hungry and the thirsty,
   the strangers and the shivering,
   those who are ill,
   and those who are in prison,
and in the exchange of the simplest of gifts,
   heartfelt and from the heart,
let us realize your domain among us.
We pray this after the pattern of Jesus
   and in the power of the Spirit
   and in the promise of glory.

Year B

Mysterious Presence,
   whose kingship is most strange
   and offensive to our natural selves,
open our eyes that we may see you,
   not arrayed in signs of worldly power
but in the embrace of friends,
   in the banquet where all are equal,
   and in the laughter of those
     whom the truth has set free.
We pray this after the pattern of Jesus
   and in the power of the Spirit
   and in the promise of glory.

THE SUNDAY NEXT BEFORE ADVENT

Year C

Living Presence of strange and unworldly power,
   shattering our thrones and pedestals,
alert us to your lasting domain,
   where forgiveness reigns,
   where beauty is revealed
     wherever we turn our eyes,
   and where truth liberates us for paradise.
We pray this after the pattern of Jesus
   and in the power of the Spirit
   and in the promise of glory.

4

Living Presence of strange power,
   still centre of a turning world,
   able to do all things well,
give us calm and rest in our hearts,
   trusting in your promise that all shall be made new,
that we may bring ourselves
   and all the powers of this world
     to serve the purposes of your greater peace.
We pray this after the pattern of Jesus
   and in the power of the Spirit,
   and in the promise of glory.

5

Living Presence of truth,
   sweeping from our minds and hearts
     our picture of you with iron fist,
     and our conviction that you are always on our side,
renew in us the vision of you
   as wise and just guardian of your people,
   curbing the power of those who would harm,
   bearing in yourself what is unresolved,

and keep us steady and true,
    that those we now perceive as our enemies
    may come to be our partners
        in the work of your creating and transforming power.
We pray this after the pattern of Jesus
    and in the power of the Spirit,
    and in the promise of glory.

6

Living Presence, strange and disturbing,
    whose ways are not our ways,
    whose power is unlike any worldly power,
bless those in high office in secular and religious life,
that they may admit their failings and fears,
    and recognize their need for forgiveness,
so that they may use their power
    to lift the oppressed,
    to temper the law with mercy,
    and to work for the common good,
always holding before their eyes
    the vision of your commonwealth,
where your way rules in every heart
    and in every public place.
We pray this after the pattern of Jesus
    and in the power of the Spirit
    and in the promise of glory.

Appendix 1

A sample order of service for Holy Communion from the books of the Church of England and the Church in Wales drawing on the resources of this book for the First Sunday of Advent Year A

[Where there are alternatives, a prayer from the Church in Wales is first, a prayer from the Church of England is second.]

The Welcome

The welcome ends with this invitation to worship:

May our gift of love in worship be offered
in the name of the God whose best name is Love,
in the name of the Father and of the Son and of the Holy Spirit.
  Amen.
Let us keep silence.

Silence, after which we stand for the first hymn.

The Greeting

Grace, mercy, and peace
from God our Father and the Lord Jesus Christ
be with you,
and also with you.

The first candle of Advent will be lit, followed by this prayer:

Blessed are you, Living God,
who was and who is and who is come.

As you called Abraham and Sarah,
Isaac and Jacob, and all our ancestors of faith,
to live by your light and follow your way,
journeying in the hope of your promises,
so may we be obedient to your call.
and be ready and watchful to receive you,
vulnerable infant, crucified stranger,
risen lord, and unfailing friend,
our light, our healing, and our liberation.
To you be praise and glory for ever.

Maranatha!
Come, universal Christ, come soon!

Prayer of Preparation

Let us pray.

We sit or kneel to pray.

Father of glory, **holy and eternal,**
look upon us now in power and mercy.
May your strength overcome our weakness,
your radiance transform our blindness,
and your Spirit draw us to that love
shown and offered to us by your Son,
our Saviour Jesus Christ.
Amen.

Or:

Almighty God,
to whom all hearts are open,
all desires known,
and from whom no secrets are hidden,
cleanse the thoughts of our hearts
by the inspiration of your Holy Spirit,
that we may perfectly love you,
and worthily magnify your holy name;
through Christ our Lord.
Amen.

Prayers of Penitence

We have been afraid of the fierceness of your love,
which sears our hearts as with a laser.

Kyrie eleison.
Kyrie eleison.

We have refused to believe that you are gentle in judgement,
that you embrace our hearts with compassion.

Christe eleison.
Christe eleison.

We have failed to see that your eyes are wise in discernment,
that your justice restores and heals.

Kyrie eleison.
Kyrie eleison.

Silence

Heavenly Father,
we have sinned in thought, word and deed,
and we have failed to do what we ought to have done.

We are sorry and truly repent.
For the sake of your Son Jesus Christ who died for us,
forgive us all that is past,
and lead us in his way to walk as children of light.
Amen.

Or:

Father eternal,
giver of light and grace,
we have sinned against you and against our neighbour,
in what we have thought,
in what we have said and done,
through ignorance, through weakness,
through our own deliberate fault.
We have wounded your love,
and marred your image in us.
We are sorry and ashamed,
and repent of all our sins.
For the sake of your Son Jesus Christ,
who died for us,
forgive us all that is past;
and lead us out from darkness
to walk as children of light.
Amen.

Almighty God,
who forgives all who truly repent,
have mercy upon you,
pardon and deliver you from all your sins,
confirm and strengthen you in all goodness,
and keep you in life eternal;
through Jesus Christ our Lord.
Amen.

We stand and say the Gloria in Excelsis.

Glory to God in the highest,
and peace to his people on earth.
Lord God, heavenly King,
almighty God and Father,
we worship you,
we give you thanks,
we praise you for your glory.
Lord Jesus Christ,
only Son of the Father,
Lord God, Lamb of God,
you take away the sin of the world:
have mercy on us;
you are seated at the right hand of the Father:
receive our prayer.
For you alone are the Holy One,
you alone are the Lord,
you alone are the Most High, Jesus Christ,
with the Holy Spirit,
in the glory of God the Father. Amen.

We remain standing for the prayer for this Sunday, the Collect:

Almighty God,
give us grace to cast away the works of darkness
and to put on the armour of light,
now in the time of this mortal life,
in which your Son Jesus Christ came to us in great humility,
that on the last day,
when he shall come again in his glorious majesty
   to judge the living and the dead,
we may rise to the life immortal;
through him who is alive and reigns with you,
in the unity of the Holy Spirit,
one God, now and for ever. **Amen.**

APPENDIX I

The Liturgy of the Word

The readings from the lectionary follow.

Between readings come a psalm or canticle or hymn, this being one suggestion for this Sunday.

From the stump of an old gnarled tree,
a new shoot will yet spring forth.
From roots hidden deep in the ground,
a sapling will grow again.

The Spirit of God will rest upon you,
the spirit of wisdom and understanding,
the spirit of counsel and might,
the spirit of knowledge and godly fear.

You will not judge by what your ears hear,
nor decide by what your eyes see.
You will judge the poor with justice,
and defend the humble of the land with equity.

Your mouth will be a rod to strike down the ruthless,
and with a word you will devastate the wicked.
Round your waist you will wear the belt of justice,
and good faith will be the girdle round your body.

Then the wolf will dwell with the sheep,
and the leopard will lie down with the kid;
the calf and the young lion will grow up together,
and a little child will lead them.

The cow and the bear will feed
and their young will lie down together.
The lion will eat straw like cattle;
the infant will play over the hole of the cobra,
and the young child dance over the viper's nest.

They will not hurt or destroy in all your holy mountain,
**for the earth will be full of the knowledge of God
as the waters cover the sea.**

Here is a suggested Gospel Acclamation:

Alleluia, alleluia, alleluia.
Alleluia, alleluia, alleluia.

Keep awake. Be alert.
Open your eyes – look – and see!
Open your ears – listen – and hear!
Keep awake. Be alert.
You do not know when the time will come.
Alleluia, alleluia, alleluia.

A reading from the Gospel according to Matthew

Alleluia, alleluia, alleluia.

Matthew 24.36–44

Give glory to the living God.
Alleluia, alleluia, alleluia.

The reader turns to the preacher and says:

Unfold the Living Word for us today.

The sermon

The Creed, one of the shorter alternatives

Prayers of Intercession or Solidarity

APPENDIX I

The Liturgy of the Sacrament

We do not presume
to come to this your table, merciful Lord,
trusting in our own righteousness,
but in your manifold and great mercies.
We are not worthy to gather up the crumbs under your table.
But you are the same Lord,
whose nature is always to have mercy.
Grant us, therefore, gracious Lord,
so to eat the flesh of your dear Son Jesus Christ,
and to drink his blood,
that we may evermore dwell in him and he in us. Amen.

The Peace

You are invited to share a clasp of the hand with those near you,
to use the phrase, 'The peace of Christ',
and to resist sharing news until after the service.
We are exchanging the peace of Christ,
and this we can wish each and all,
whether we know one another or not,
and whether we get on with one another or not.

A hymn is sung

The Preparation of the Table

Blessed are you, eternal God, Source of all creation.
Through your goodness we have this bread to offer,
which earth has given and human hands have made.
It will become for us the Bread of Life.
Blessed be God for ever.

Blessed are you, eternal God, Source of all creation.
Through your goodness we have this wine to offer,
fruit of the vine and work of human hands.
It will become for us the Lifeblood of the World.
Blessed be God for ever.

Blessed are you, eternal God, Source of all creation.
Through your goodness we have ourselves to offer,
gift of the womb and shaped by human hands.
We will become for you a Living Body.
Blessed be God for ever.

The Thanksgiving Prayer

The Giving of Communion

Draw near with faith.
Receive the Body of our Lord Jesus Christ which was given for you,
and his Blood which was shed for you.
Remember that he died for you and lives for you,
and feed on him in your hearts by faith with thanksgiving.

Come, receive who you are.
Become what you see.

On a church door there was this notice:
Everybody is welcome to receive communion here.
Only one thing is asked of each and all of us, that we be hungry.
However, some people prefer to come to the altar for a blessing:
if so, please incline your head rather than holding out your hands.
Or you may prefer to sit quietly where you are.
May there always be pillars to hide behind for the shy, the puzzled, and those who are searching and seeking.

APPENDIX I

After Communion

We remain sitting or kneeling in silence after communion, the silence ending with this prayer, which you may wish to use each day this week.

Living Presence of truth,
 whose word resounds
  amid the clamour of our violence,
keep your households watchful,
 aware of the hour in which we live,
and hasten the day when the sounds of war
 will be for ever stilled,
the powers of evil scattered,
and the earth and its peoples gathered into one.
We pray this through the One
 in whose constant coming we trust,
  whose day is always near.

Father of all,
**we give you thanks and praise,
that when we were still far off
you met us in your Son and brought us home.
Dying and living, he declared your love,
gave us grace, and opened the gate of glory.
May we who share Christ's body live his risen life,
we who drink his cup bring life to others,
we whom the Spirit lights give light to the world.
Keep us firm in the hope you have set before us,
so that we and all your children shall be free,
and the whole earth live to praise your name;
through Christ our Lord. Amen.**

Going Forth

We stand for the last hymn.
We remain standing for the Blessing:

Christ the Sun of Righteousness shine upon you,
and scatter the darkness from before your path;
and the blessing of God almighty,
the Father, the Son, and the Holy Spirit,
be among you and remain with you always.
Amen.

Go in peace to love and serve the Lord.
In the name of Christ. Amen.

Appendix 2

A sample order of service for Morning Prayer from the books of the Church in Wales and the Church of England drawing upon the resources of this book for the Sunday between 3 and 9 July, Year A

Morning Acclamation

Grace, mercy, and peace
from God our Father
and the Lord Jesus Christ
be with you
and also with you.

We have come together in the name of Christ
to offer our praise and thanksgiving,
to hear and receive God's holy word,
to pray for the needs of the world,
and to seek the forgiveness of our sins,
that by the power of the Holy Spirit
we may give ourselves to the service of God.

The night has passed,
and the day lies open before us;
let us pray with one heart and mind.

Silence

As we rejoice in the gift of this new day,
so may the light of your presence, O God,
set our hearts on fire with love for you,
now and for ever.
Amen.

Blessed are you, Lord our God,
creator and redeemer of all;
to you be glory and praise for ever.
From the waters of chaos you drew forth the world
and in your great love fashioned us in your image.
Now, through the deep waters of death,
you have brought your people to new birth
by raising your Son to life in triumph.
May Christ your light ever dawn in our hearts
as we offer you our sacrifice of thanks and praise.
Blessed be God, Father, Son, and Holy Spirit:
Blessed be God for ever.

Penitence

Our Lord Jesus Christ said:
'The first commandment is this:
Love the Lord your God with all your heart, with all your soul,
with all your mind and with all your strength.
The second is this:
Love your neighbour as yourself.
There is no other commandment greater than these.'
Amen. Lord have mercy.

Kyries

We have become bloated balloons: puncture us.
Kyrie eleison.
We have become full of ourselves: empty us.
Christe eleison.

We have missed one another by miles: focus us.
Kyrie eleison.

Silence

Lord our God,
in our sin we have avoided your call.
Our love for you is like a morning cloud,
like the dew that goes away early.
Have mercy on us;
deliver us from judgement;
bind up our wounds and revive us
in Jesus Christ our Lord. Amen.

May the Lord grant us
pardon and remission of all our sins,
time for amendment of life,
and the grace and comfort of the Holy Spirit.
Amen.

A hymn of praise and thanksgiving

The Ministry of the Word

Psalm

An unfolding of part of Psalm 145

The beat of your heart,
reliable and steady,
the voice of your faithfulness.
**The beat of your heart,
reliable and steady,
the voice of your faithfulness.**

For the cry of the baby,
for the flowering of youth,
for the strength of maturity,
we give thanks to our God.
**The beat of your heart,
reliable and steady,
the voice of your faithfulness.**
For laws that protect us,
for those on alert,
for the routines of safety,
we give thanks to our God.
**The beat of your heart,
reliable and steady,
the voice of your faithfulness.**
For the trust of friends,
for the blessings of home,
for the covenants of love,
we give thanks to our God.
**The beat of your heart,
reliable and steady,
the voice of your faithfulness.**

The Old Testament reading

Before the reading:
A reading from the book of the prophet Zechariah
(chapter 9, verses 9 to 12)

After the reading:
Hear what the Spirit is saying to the Church.
Thanks be to God.

Or:

Here ends the Old Testament reading.

Silence

A response

The Sixth Commandment

You shall not commit murder.
Reverence all life.
Live at peace with everyone:
overcome evil with good.

Take your neighbour to your heart;
welcome the stranger in your midst.
Be generous and hospitable,
with your time, round your table.
Deepen your respect, one for another,
receive your guests as you would wish to be received.

Silence

You shall not commit murder.
Reverence all life.
Live at peace with everyone:
overcome evil with good.

The New Testament reading

Before the reading:
A reading from the letter of Paul to the Romans
(chapter 7, verses 15 to 25a)

Or:

A reading from the Gospel according to Matthew
(chapter 11, verses 16 to 19, and 25 to 30)

After the reading:
Hear what the Spirit is saying to the Church.
Thanks be to God.

Or:

Here ends the New Testament reading.

Silence

An unfolding of the Benedictus

We praise you, God of freedom,
releasing all who are imprisoned,
raising up for us a powerful deliverer,
a descendant of God's servant David.

Such was your promise, long, long ago,
by the lips of your holy prophets,
that you would free us from the grip of evil,
from the powers that ensnare us.

This was your covenant of old,
that you would treat us with justice and compassion,
that we might serve you without fear,
truthful and courageous our whole life long.

John, forerunner, from the womb you were called
to be a prophet to prepare God's way,
going before the Liberator who will lead us to our freedom,
disarming the powers of evil and opening the prison doors.

For in the tender mercies of our God
the rising sun has burst upon our lives,
giving light to those who dwell in darkness and in the shadow
   of death,
and guiding our feet into ways of peace.

The Creed

Let us declare our faith in God.

We believe in God the Father,
from whom every family
in heaven and on earth is named.

We believe in God the Son,
who lives in our hearts through faith,
and fills us with his love.

We believe in God the Holy Spirit,
who strengthens us
with power from on high.

We believe in one God,
Father, Son, and Holy Spirit.
Amen.

The Prayers

The Lord's Prayer

As our Saviour taught us, we boldly pray:
Our Father who art in heaven,
hallowed be thy name,
thy kingdom come,
thy will be done,
on earth as it is in heaven.
Give us this day our daily bread.
And forgive us our trespasses
as we forgive those
who trespass against us.
And lead us not into temptation,
but deliver us from evil.
For thine is the kingdom,

the power and the glory,
for ever and ever. Amen.

The Collects

The prayer for the fourth Sunday after Trinity

O God, the protector of all who trust in you,
without whom nothing is strong, nothing is holy,
increase and multiply upon us your mercy,
that with you as our ruler and guide
we may so pass through things temporal
that we lose not the things eternal;
grant this, heavenly Father,
for our Lord Jesus Christ's sake,
who is alive and reigns with you,
in the unity of the Holy Spirit,
one God, now and for ever.

The prayer for peace

O God, the author of peace and lover of concord,
to know you is eternal life,
to serve you is perfect freedom:
defend us in all assaults of our enemies,
that we, surely trusting in your protection,
may not fear the power of any adversaries;
through Jesus Christ our Lord. **Amen.**

The prayer for grace

Eternal God and Father,
by your power we are created
and by your love we are redeemed:
guide and strengthen us by your Spirit,
that we may give ourselves to you
in love and service of one another;
through Jesus Christ our Lord. **Amen.**

A hymn

A homily

Prayer for others

A hymn

Final Prayers

Living Presence, folly to worldly ways,
    just and compassionate in your rule,
    revealing the strength of love
        by being born a vulnerable child
        and by dying a nailtorn outcast,
turn our eyes and desires
    from the seductions and trappings of worldly power,
and give us the strength
    to risk being vulnerable ourselves,
that we may learn how to become
    truly wise and divinely human.
We pray this after the pattern of Jesus
    and in the power of the Spirit.

The Peace

May the peace of God,
which passes all understanding,
keep our hearts and minds in Christ Jesus.
Amen.

The Shalom of Christ be with you.
The Peace of the Living One enfold you.

Appendix 3

Praying for Others
The Prayer of Solidarity
commonly called Intercession

Suggested Frameworks and Samples

An Introduction

Let us greet those for whom we are about to pray:
We hold you to our hearts.
We hold you to the heart of *name(s) of saints* ...
We hold you to the heart of the Beloved Disciple.
We hold you to the heart of Mary.
We hold you to the heart of Jesus the Christ, the Universal One.
We hold you to the heart of the Mystery with love.

For each Section

Each of the following sections may start with
We bring into mind's eye and heart's care ...

Each section may end with
Your kingdom come: **Your will be done.**
or
Your will be done: **Your love be shown.**
or
Holy wisdom: **Abundant blessing.**

APPENDIX 3

The Sections

[Three dots ... indicate places to pause for, say, ten seconds' silence.]

The people, homes, and work of this parish ... the local council ... those who live at/in *names of houses or streets* ...

Our families and friends ... those who work as *names of jobs* ...

The people of this county of N/this city of N ... all who live in N (ward, area, neighbourhood) ... the county/city council, N our councillor ...

This diocese of N, N our Area Dean, N our Archdeacon, and N our bishop ... N archbishop of N ... the people of the province of N in the Anglican Communion ... the leaders and people of the other churches, particulary N ...

The people of Ireland and of the United Kingdom, the Parliaments and Assemblies, Elizabeth our Queen, N our MP ...

The people of Europe, particularly those who live in N (country), and N our Member of the European Parliament ...

The people of *name(s) of countries in the other continents of the world* ...

Places and people who are troubled ... *names* ...
and those who seek to repair the damage ... *names* ...
those among us, *names* ... , *those for whom prayer has been asked here* ... , and those who care for them.

Those who have died, *names* ... , and those whose year's mind falls at this time, *names* ...

APPENDIX 3

A Concluding Prayer

From the Source deep within each one of us,
with the energy of the Great Spirit, the Holy Spirit,
   at work between us and among us,
after the pattern and in the name of Jesus,
   we breathe towards you
      wisdom – sophia,
      justice – well-being – shalom,
      love that is heart-felt and mind-full,
      steady and strong-willed,
      a costly gift, again and again,
      to bring laughter and life in abundance.

Two Samples

[The first sample can be found in Appendix 4, on p. 358.]

Here is the second sample, each section expanding from the local towards the global. The details of course depend on where the user lives.

We bring into mind's eye and heart's care
those who serve this community at the school ...
and at the Whistling Sands Café ...
those who live at Morfa Bach in Aberdaron ...
Pen y Maes Bellaf in Uwchmynydd ...
2 Glanrafon Cottage in Rhoshirwaun ...
the people of this place, among them NN ...

We bring into mind's eye and heart's care here
on Pen Lleyn the people of Abersoch ...
those who care for the streams and rivers of this peninsula ...
in this county and diocese the people of Aberdyfi ...
and of Llandudno Junction ...

APPENDIX 3

We bring into mind's eye and heart's care,
in their daily life and work,
abbots and abbesses ...
exorcists ...
palaeontologists ...
understudies ...

We bring into mind's eye and heart's care
the people of the town of Aberaeron and the surrounding countryside in Dyfed in southwestern Wales ...
the people of the Chiltern Hills in southern England ...
the people of the town of Harrogate and the surrounding countryside in North Yorkshire in northern England ...
the people of the city of Milton Keynes and its hinterland in Buckinghamshire in southern England ...
the people of the town of Sherborne and the surrounding countryside in Dorset in southwestren England ...
the people of the area of Woolwich in London ...

We bring into mind's eye and heart's care,
in continental Europe,
the people of the city of Aarhus and its
hinterland in Denmark ...
and the city of Sofia and its hinterland in Bulgaria ...
and around the world
the people of the city of Aba Ukpo and its hinterland in Akwa Ibom State in southeastern Nigeria in West Africa ...
the people of the sea of Galilee in the Middle East ...
the people of the city of Nasik and its hinterland in Maharashta in India in southern Asia ...
the people of the city of Ulsan and its hinterland in South Korea in eastern Asia ...

Appendix 4

An experimental order of service for the Blessed Communion

Ecumenical and Universal

Here Comes Everybody

Everybody is welcome
to receive communion here.
One thing only is asked of all of us:
that we be hungry.

[Square brackets indicate material that can be omitted]

Welcome

[To the universe beyond and within us, and to this planet earth,
to this continent of Europe and to these Atlantic Isles,
to Pen Lleyn and Aberdaron,
to our visitors and to Hywyn's People,
croeso, welcome.]

Welcome in the communion of the Holy Spirit.
Welcome in the fiercely loving justice of Jesus of Nazareth.
Welcome in the name of the wise, compassionate Creator.
Those who are hungry, welcome.
Those who are thirsty, welcome.

[Hymn]

Approach

Eternal and most loving One,
in whom we live and move and have our being,
open our minds and hearts,
our flesh and feelings,
touch even the deepest places
and the truths as yet unnamed,
in each one of us, unique and precious,
and in all of us, bound together in your love.

Refining Flame, burn into us.
Cleansing Wind, scour through us.
Fountain of Water, well up within us.
Living Word, breathe through us.
Living Body, touch us and heal us.
Living Bread, nourish us.
Lifeblood of the world, surge through us. Amen.

[Bringing into the Present our Birth and our Baptism]

[The declaring of names]

Living mysterious Presence,
beyond our power to control,
Living One of many names,
Loving One of Justice and Intimacy,
revealed to us in Jesus,
you have called each and all of us by name.

We remember our names:
the name we have inherited from the past,
from our ancestors in time immemorial;
the name we were given by those who first nurtured us;
the name we are invited to choose as we follow the Way of
 Jesus.

Let each of us tell our names to those around us ...

Or:

Let us tell our names, one by one,
to this company now gathered ...

Names are said aloud.

We are dearly loved ...
We belong together for ever in the One who names us ...
who will give each of us a white stone,
with a new name written on the stone,
known only to the one who receives it.

[The Blessing of Water]

Water is poured into font or bowl.

Here is the water of our survival day by day, drawn up as from a well ...

Here are the waters that were broken to give us birth ...

Here is the water that flows so often hidden underground ...

Here is the water that purifies, scours, and cleanses us of all that is toxic ...

Here is the water of refreshment and pleasure, of fountain, fall, and pool ...

Here is the water of raging power, of tidal wave and destroying flood ...

Here is the water that draws back and allows us to pass dry shod ...

Here is the water of the Jordan river, of the passage from slavery and oppression to the freedom of a promised land ...

Here is the water of eternal life, bubbling cheerfully as an ever-flowing spring ...

Here is the water of buoyancy, of the ocean of divine love ...

Here is the water of chaos and the creatures of the profound unknown, the roaring wind and fearful silence ...

Here is the water of drowning, of the death of grasping self, of the decay of flesh and blood ...

Here is the water of dying, bearing us across the ancient river ...

Here is the water that is the simplest gift to the thirsty, and that washes the weary traveller's feet ...

Here is the water that springs up in barren ground to our unexpected joy ...

Here is the water that flows for the healing of the nations ...

Living Creator,
bless this water and bless us who are touched by it.
We ask a blessing in the name of the Creator,
    the Life-Giver, Father-Mother of us all;
we ask a blessing in the name of the Redeemer,
    the Pain-Bearer, the Son;
we ask a blessing in the name of the Sanctifier,
    the Love-Maker, the Holy Spirit.

The Living One is within us – the Holy Spirit.
The Living One is among us – the Presence of Christ.
The Living One is beyond us – the Creator.

Bringing all three together in a spiral,
we bless our neighbours on the forehead.

A small bowl of water scooped from the larger bowl is passed from hand to hand, each in turn blessing the next person.

Recognition 1

Each week has three sentences particular to that occasion. The sung Kyries below may be used after each of them, or the short said response may be used.

KYR–I–E YE–SU CHRI—STE

HU–I–OS THE–OU E–LEI—SON

After the first line: **Kyrie eleison.**
After the second line: **Christe eleison.**
After the third line: **Kyrie eleison.**

The Spirit of compassion is moving among us …
The Spirit of forgiveness is filling our hearts …
The Spirit of reconciliation is flowing into our lives …

The Spirit of Christ is rescuing us, liberating us.
The Spirit of Christ is repairing us, healing us.
The Spirit of Christ is restoring us a hundredfold.

The Spirit of justice makes right what is wrong.
The Spirit of truth shrivels the lie.
The Spirit of love pours out in torrents.

The Holy Spirit takes human shape among us.
So let it be for us. Amen.

Or:

Recognition 2

Let us become aware of the failings of humankind,
our own, those we hear about, and those we collude with …

Let us become aware of those who wield more power than we do,
those we scapegoat and blame, imagining them sitting beside us now …

We bring them and we bring ourselves
to the searing healing power of the Loving One …

Silence

Loving One, you accept us, you cleanse us, you give us new life.
You call us to your service and friendship.

But we have wounded your love and marred your image.
We have wandered far in a land that is waste.

The sung Kyries on the previous page may be used here.

From all our corporate and personal failures,
from those to which we are blind,
and from those we cannot now remember,
we turn to you, wounded One,
in repentance and in trust.

Forgiveness and Reconciliation

[True love, divine love, is sure and steady,
absorbing our hurt, never deflected by it,
accepting tragedy and redeeming it,
involved with us, closer to us than breathing,
exposed and vulnerable to everything we do.
**True love, divine love,
gladly accepts the truths of our hearts,
runs with delight to embrace us,
favours us at the banquet of joy.**
Jesus Christ embodied that love and calls us to embody it too.
To those who promised to weave its pattern, the Spirit was given,
to forgive or withhold forgiveness,
to enable or defer the forgiveness of the One
who is always waiting to receive us with open arms ...]

In the name of Christ, aware of the gift of forgiveness,
embodying the Gospel of unconditional love,
with the voice of Christ resonating within us, let us say,
     each to all,
I forgive you.
So let us be assured that we are forgiven, forgiven by Christ,
forgiven by our fellow-pilgrims, released from all that hurts us.
Amen. Thanks be to God.
Let us live together in the reconciliation wrought by the Living One
and in the Shalom that is the divine will for the universe.
The Peace of Christ be with you.
The Shalom of the Living One encompass you.

*We pass the Peace one to another in turn,
letting our eyes move round the company,
focusing on each person as he or she receives the greeting.*

Gloria

Glorious One, we give you worship –
peace to those who love you well –
adoration from your people –
thankfulness our voices tell.

Yes, we bless you for your glory,
full of light and truth and grace,
Word made flesh in Christ incarnate,
shining through a human face.

Born in cave and killed on gibbet,
outcast dying in disgrace,
burned by fires of human hatred,
raised by love's fierce last embrace.

You alone are Love most holy,
you alone great deeds have done,
intimate in wondrous glory,
in the Spirit, Three-in-One.

The Unfolding of the Word

Prayer

Holy Spirit, wisdom discerning,
guide our searching, speak to our listening,
challenge us with your questioning, hold us in silence,
whisper to our hearts' understanding,
unfold the truths that set us free.

Reading

Psalm

Reading

Gospel Acclamation

A-LE-LU A   A-LE-LU A   A-LE - LU - IA

Gospel

[Homily]

Collect for the day

A Way of Believing

Yes – I trust in AbbaAmma,
source of all that comes to be,
goodness, truth, and marvellous beauty,
surging life – Love's mystery.

Yes – I trust in Love embodied,
Jesus born in Galilee,
healing outcasts, eating with them,
crucified upon the Tree,

bearing pain with all creation,
willing love to victory,
loosening evil's grip for ever,
death no more the enemy.

Foe and friend, in Love's acceptance,
each and all alike are formed,
freed by touch and word and water,
fed by bread and wine transformed.

Yes – I trust the hidden Spirit
in and through our common life
weaving threads all torn and broken,
shaping justice out of strife.

Yes – I trust in Love's communion,
lover, loved, and mutual friend,
seated at the welcoming table,
gently bidding us attend.

Prayers of Solidarity

Eternal and most loving One,
in whose presence we live the nights and days,
the darkness and the light,
by whose creative power we are sustained,
we call to mind and heart your world and your people,
that through our prayer you would bless them.

Strengthen the worldwide communion of churches
that we may serve you more faithfully.
Bless ...
May those who confess your name be united in your truth,
live together in your love, and reveal your glory in the world.
Living One, your will be done:
Your love be shown.

Bless and guide the powers that be, give wisdom to all in authority,
to those who administer the law, and to those who seek to reform it,
to the United Nations, to the international courts of law.
Bless ...
Guide this and every land in the ways of justice and peace,
that we may honour one another and seek the common good.
Living One, your will be done:
Your love be shown.

Give grace to us, our families and friends,
to our neighbours, to this parish,
and to all the people of this neighbourhood/village/town/city/
   county.
Bless ...
Give us a generous heart to love as Christ loves us.
Living One, your will be done:
Your love be shown.

Comfort and heal all those who suffer
the hurts of others' words and deeds,
the pains of flesh and feeling,
the bewilderments of dread and anxiety,
the despair of days and nights without meaning.
Bless ...
Give them courage and hope in their troubles,
bring them the joy of your salvation,
and give to those who care for them grace and skill to do your
   healing work.
Living One, your will be done:
Your love be shown.

Hear us as we remember those who have died,
whether in faith or doubt, in trust or terror,
all whose deep desires are known to you alone.
Bless ...
Spread over them your peace and healing grace,
and unite us with them in your good time.
Living One, your will be done:
Your love be shown.

Rejoicing in the fellowship of *NN*,
and of all the holy fools of God,
we commend ourselves and all people to your unfailing love.
Living One,
your will be done throughout the universe:
Your love shine forth in glory.

Praying in Christ

Abba, our Father,
Amma, our Mother,
Beloved, our Friend,
Creator of all:
your name be held holy,
your domain spread among us,
your wisdom be our guide,
your way be our path,
your will be done well,
at all times, in all places,
on earth as in heaven.
Give us the bread
we need for today,
the manna of your promise,
the bread of your tomorrow.
As we release those
indebted to us,
so forgive us our debts,
our trespass on others.
Fill us with courage
in time of our testing.
Spare us from trials
too severe to endure.
Free us from the grip
of the powers that bind.
For yours is the goodness
in which evil dissolves;
yours is the joy
that sounds through the pain;
yours is the life
which swallows up death.
Yours is the glory,
the transfiguring light,
the victory of love,
for time and eternity,

for age after age.
So be it. Amen.

[Hymn]

At the Taking of the Bread and Wine 1

We bring to this place our living and our dying.
We bring our trust and and our doubt.
We bring our friends and our enemies.
We bring the bread that sustains us.
We bring the wine that mellows us.

We bring what has already been changed
grain and seed, flour and grape,
baked and pressed, loaf and vintage.

We bring our substance:
flesh-bodies, touching and being touched,
life-blood, circulating and flowing.

We bring our loving:
    yearning and broken,
    desiring greater intimacy,
    longing for greater justice,
    knowing that if we do not love one another we shall die.

All is gift.
All is grace.

Here may we find the transforming fire.
Here may we find life for the body.

Let us be thankful.
Let us open ourselves to be transformed.

Or:

At the Taking of the Bread and Wine 2

Blessed are you, eternal One, Source of all creation,
through your goodness we have this bread to bring to you,
which earth has given and human hands have made:
it will become for us the Bread of Life:
Blessed be the Living One for ever.

Blessed are you, eternal One, Source of all creation,
through your goodness we have this wine to bring to you,
fruit of the vine and work of human hands:
it will become for us the Lifeblood of the World:
Blessed be the Living One for ever.

Blessed are you, eternal One, Source of all creation:
through your goodness we have ourselves to bring to you,
gift of the womb and shaped by human hands:
we will become for you a Living Body:
Blessed be the Living One for ever.

The Thanksgiving Prayer 1

The Loving One is in the midst of us:
The Holy Spirit dwells among us.

We surrender our hearts to our faithful Creator:
We open them to the Living One and to one another.

Let us give thanks for the wonder of the divine glory,
for the gift of this our planet, beautiful and fragile in the
 heavens,
for our responsibility as guardians of all that is being created,
for the vision of one human commonwealth,
with peace known on earth and goodwill shared among all
 people ...

APPENDIX 4

Drawn by the magnet of the Living One
ever closer in the Presence of the Mystery,
we adore the Creator who gives us life.

Let us give thanks for Jesus of Nazareth,
living the truth of us and the truth of the Living One,
glad to be born of Mary to dwell with us,
a human being most wonderfully alive,
yet enduring to the end and dying as the means of our
 reconciliation and our healing,
who is most gloriously risen, the pioneer of our salvation ...

Drawn by the magnet of the Suffering One
ever closer in the Presence of the Mystery,
**we embrace the Christ who bears our pain
and makes us whole.**

Let us give thanks for the Holy Spirit,
moving invisibly deep within us,
spinning the thread of attention among us,
bringing to life in us the Way and Wisdom of Jesus,
nurturing us with the food of the Living One,
and with the fountain of water that wells up to eternal life,
sending us into the heart of the conflicts of the world,
to speak the words and live the lives of justice and of peace,
of truth and of healing ...

Drawn by the magnet of the Loving One,
ever closer in the Presence of the Mystery,
**we give thanks for the Spirit
who makes love with us
in the dance of the new creation.**

So let us give thanks to the Living One for accepting us in the
 Beloved,
who in the night of loneliness and desolation, of agony and
 betrayal,

took the bread that sustains us all, gave thanks, and broke it,
and gave it to his disciples and said,
**Take, eat, this is my Body,
my Living Presence, given for you:
do this to re-member me,
to bring us together in the world.**
In the same way he took the cup of wine,
the wine of our sorrow and our solace,
gave thanks, and gave it to them and said,
**Drink of this, all of you, this is my Blood,
my Very Life, spent for you:
do this to re-member me,
to bring us alive in the world.**

Silence

Creator Spirit, as we celebrate the one great sacrifice of love,
hover now over your people, over this bread and wine,
that they may be to us the Body and Blood of Christ.

For in the mystery of faith,
**Christ has died,
Christ is risen,
Christ is here,
Christ will come.**

And now with all who have ever lived,
with saints and martyrs and forgotten faithful people,
with angels and archangels and all the heavenly company,
with all who are alive and all who are yet to be born,
with all creation in all time, with joy we sing:

to the tune Nicaea

**Holy! Holy! Holy! beating heart of glory,
all your works shall praise your name in earth and sky and sea!
Holy! Holy! Holy! strong in love and mercy,
living communion, blessed Trinity!**

Blessed is the Anointed who comes in the Name of the Living
  One!
Hosanna in the Highest!

Alleluia! Glory and Splendour, both human and divine!
So be it! Amen!

Or:

The Thanksgiving Prayer 2

[Let us contemplate in wonder, awe, and gratitude
the universe of which we are a part,
the vast expanse of interstellar space,
galaxies, suns, the planets in their courses,
and this beautiful and fragile earth our island home ...

Let us with dignified humility accept our vocation
  to be trustees of all that lives and breathes under the sun,
to be skilful in probing the mysteries of creation,
to be wise and reverent in our use of the resources of the
  earth ...]

So let us greet the Living One who is within us and beyond us:

Creator Spirit, energy inspiring,
brooding over the formless deeps,
wings outstretched in the primal dark,
enclosing and calling forth all that has come to be,
ever present to renew and re-create ...

beckoning all that is chaotic and without form –
the spontaneous leap of microscopic particles,
the isolated impulse of the human heart –
weaving them into the pattern of a larger whole ...

urging forward into ever more complex forms of life …

planting an awareness and faint yearning for the unattained …

challenging a choosing of the unknown yet to be,
a risk that is a dying that a fuller life be born,
a sacrifice of lesser ways, a giving up of slaughter,
the law of gentleness in the midst of force and fury …

a way made known to us by Jesus of Nazareth,
eternal persuasive love made visible at last …
the love that through the aeons of unrecorded time
has striven and suffered, died and risen to new life,
within the very fabric of the universe,
accepting us so deeply that we need no longer seize and possess
 out of malice and of fear,
clearing the way for us to be empowered
to mend creation's threads that have been torn,
to make the desert bloom
and the trees to grow again on barren ground …
So we take the produce of this earth,
the bread of our sustenance,
the wine of our solace and our sorrow,
as Jesus invited us to do,
that we might know Creator Spirit transfiguring our flesh and
 blood
 to a glory that we but dimly sense,
filling us with the living presence, the very self, of Jesus,
given, sacrificed for us,
to bring us alive, to bring us together as one body.

For he took bread, gave thanks,
broke it, and gave it to his disciples and said,
Take, eat, this is my Body which is given for you;
do this to re-member me.

APPENDIX 4

In the same way, after supper, he took a cup of wine,
gave thanks, and gave it to them and said,
Drink of this, all of you,
this is my Blood which is shed for you:
do this, as often as you drink it, to re-member me.

Creator Spirit, as we celebrate the one great sacrifice of love,
hover now over your people,
over this bread and wine,
that they may be to us the Body and Blood of Christ.
For in the mystery of faith,
Christ has died, Christ is risen,
Christ is here, Christ will come.
Through Christ, with Christ, in Christ,
by the power and in the presence of Creator Spirit,
with all that lives throughout the universe, seen and unseen,
we worship you, eternal Mystery of Love,
in songs of everlasting praise:

to the tune Nicaea:

Holy! Holy! Holy! beating heart of glory!
all your works shall praise your name in earth and sky and sea!
Holy! Holy! Holy! strong in love and mercy!
living communion, blessed Trinity!

Blessed is the Anointed who comes in the Name of the Living
 One!
Hosanna in the Highest!

Alleluia!Glory and Splendour, both human and divine!
So be it! Amen!

APPENDIX 4

The Breaking of the Bread

The bread which we break
is a sharing in the Body of Christ.
The wine which we bless
is a sharing in the Blood of Christ.
Body and Blood of one humanity,
we shall be transfigured to glory.

Agnus Dei

Lamb, human and divine, taking away the sin of the world,
having compassion upon us –
Lover, human and divine, affirming the worth of the world,
accepting us in love for ever –
Healer, human and divine, bearing the pain of the world,
giving us and all creation your peace –
pour mercy upon us, whisper your love for us, **give us peace.**

① Do - na no - bis pa - cem, pa-cem;
do - na no - bis pa - cem.

② Do - - na no - bis pa - cem,
do - na no - bis pa - - cem.

③ Do - na no - bis pa - cem,
do - na no - bis pa - - cem.

368

APPENDIX 4

The Communion 1

Let us open our hands, open our hearts,
open the hidden places of our being,
and into our deep soul-self
let there enter the heartbeat of those we love,
the lifeblood of our villages, towns, and cities,
the lifestream of the tides and currents and seasons,
the pulsing of our planet and of the stars;
let there enter all the joys and pains our cup can bear;
let us be nourished by the new life
that comes through what is broken;
and in and through it all, to transform it to glory,
let us receive the Body, the Living Presence,
the Blood, the Very Self, of Jesus,
and let us feed and live and love, in faith, with gratitude.

[Beloved, we draw near to be loved by you,
in deep yet trembling trust,
through this matter of your creation,
this material stuff of bread and body,
this fluid of wine and blood,
that your desire for us and ours for you
may be blended in deep joy and ecstasy,
that we may be enriched and doubly blessed.]

**We draw near to receive this offering of yourself,
your intimate, vulnerable, and naked body,
imparted to us, incorporated in us,
that we may dwell and love and create,
you in us and we in you.**

Receive who you are. Become what you see.

Words when giving and receiving communion:
The Body of Christ. **I am.**
The Blood of Christ. **Amen.**

Or:

The Communion 2

The Bread of Life,
Love embodied,
nourish you.
The Lifeblood,
Love expended,
enliven you.
Feed on the Living One,
full of humanity,
laced with divinity.
Feed on the Loving One,
by faith, with thanksgiving.

Words when giving and receiving communion:
The Body of Christ. **I am.**
The Blood of Christ. **Amen.**

Or:

The Communion 3

Let us receive the flesh-bread
and become one with the body of Christ.
Let us receive the blood-wine,
and become one with the life of Christ.
Let us pause between the receivings,
anticipating the separation of our flesh from our blood when
    we die,
affirming that we are willing to die in Christ, into Christ,
for the sake of the Kingdom of righteousness and justice,
thus participating in the Anointed One's self-giving way
that serves the flourishing of abundant life.

Or:

The Communion 4

We break this bread for all the peoples of faith,
so often divided by hatred and suspicion ...

we break this bread for the earth and oceans,
plundered and torn by human hands ...

we break this bread for the destitute and starving,
the grieving and the stigmatized,
and for all the broken-hearted ...

we break this bread for the wounded child within each one of us ...

that the peoples and the planet may be bound together
in the healing that is promised us,
in the freedom that from fear releases us,
in the new life that transforms us –
through these first-fruits of the harvest –
the Gift that is given, the Presence that is hidden,
in the Breaking of the Bread:
the Body of Christ, the Blood of Christ.
Come, eat, drink.
Receive who you are. Become what you see.

Words when giving and receiving communion:
The Body of Christ. **I am.**
The Blood of Christ. **Amen.**

After Communion

Ever-loving and ever-creating One,
feeding us with the Living Bread,
delighting us with the Wine of New Life,
giving us a pledge of unbounded Love,
celebrating with us the dawn of a new creation,
joining us to one another in the Mystical Body of Christ,
**we give you thanks and praise,
we offer you ourselves,
all that we have and all that we are,
and we yearn with eager longing
for the fulfilment of all things in Christ,
Alpha and Omega, our Beginning and our End.**

[The following canticle or a hymn]

The refrain after each line is:
sing of your love, now and for ever.

Living One of our ancestors' faith, we bless you ...

We bless your holy and glorious name ...

We bless you on the heights of the mountains ...

We bless you in deep and secret places ...

We bless you in songs of animals and birds ...

We bless you in the sounds of the city ...

We bless you even in the midst of distress ...

We bless you on the lips of courageous people ...

We bless you in places where justice glows ...

We bless you in the bread and the wine ...

We bless you in the Body and the Blood ...]

APPENDIX 4

The Blessing 1

The Blessing of the Living One,
Giver of Life, Bearer of Pain, Maker of Love,
flow through us to all humankind
and to the whole creation.
So be it. Amen.

Or:

The Blessing 2

The Blessing of the Living One be with us,
Father and Mother,
Sustainer of our earth,
Source of all that is and that shall be.

The Blessing of the Living One be with us,
our Messiah, our Christ,
our Risen and Glorious Loved One
and our Friend.

The Blessing of the Living One be with us,
Spirit spreading love and joy in our hearts,
giving hope to the battered ones,
inspiring justice and peace for the little ones.

**May this rich blessing be with us,
with all humankind living and departed,
and with all the creatures of land and sea and air.
May our days be long on this good earth.**

**For we have been nourished
by the Bread of Life,
we have been quickened
by the Lifeblood of the Universe.**

With courage and in hope
let us continue on the journey.

So be it. Amen.

Some Notes

Welcome to this celebration of the 'Blessed Communion', a literal translation from the Welsh 'Y Cymun Bendigaid'. The form of the service has evolved from a house celebration, and has never stayed still for long. This text is very much 'work in progress'. Any comments you may have will be appreciated.

One of the aims of this experiment is to worship in a way that is exploratory in language and style without being different every time or quirkily experimental.

There is no attempt to erase from the scriptural readings any language or content that may to our ears be offensive. The time of reflection will help us to sift the words and so discern what the Spirit of God may be revealing to us and in us today. Paintings and photographs and recorded music may also be used in this process.

The hymns and prayers are all attempts to express our aspirations and celebrations in words that connect for us today. The structure should be familiar to those who usually worship in one of the main traditions of the Christian Church.

The Peace near the beginning is fairly formal, a ritual exchange passed round the company. We are invited to look at each person as he or she receives the Peace.

We celebrate and re-present to one another the story of the life, death, and resurrection of Jesus Christ, the One who embodied in flesh and blood the Spirit of God. We actively re-member, re-embody, so as to participate, in all that we are and do, in the wonder and mystery of Love.

The drama has a producer, but we are all on stage and there is no audience. The producer's responsibility to the wider community is to enable a celebration that is authentically a

Christian Communion. But we all share the speaking parts, either by solo or in chorus. The parts we say together are in bold type. And on our behalf there is a bread-breaker and a cup-bearer to focus our attention on the bread and wine at appropriate points, and to begin our sharing of the sacrament.

If you are used to addressing a large number of people in schools or churches or elsewhere, please note that we are a smaller gathering. We try to blend our voices when speaking or singing together, so that we may sound as one, and even begin to act as one.

We gather in the shape of a horseshoe. The circle needs to be incomplete and open to the beyond – both of the wider world and of God.

We need to be free at any time to focus our eyes on the words, on others, on the bread and wine, on the cross, on the ikon. Times of silence are therefore part of the worship.

A book is available which gives an account of the background and context of the various parts of the service: *Love Re-membered: Resources for a House Eucharist*. It is published by Cairns Publications and costs £5, plus £2 for post and packing. The book does not include a continuous script such as you have in your hands. If you would like to make copies of what you are now holding, a copyright fee of £10 gives permission to make up to twenty. Cheques should be made out to Jim Cotter. Correspondence should be addressed to Gernant, Aberdaron, Pwllheli, Gwynedd, LL58 8BG. All being well later this year, the book should be available for download from my website, www.cottercairns.co.uk

If you have the responsibility of facilitating a celebration using this script, I do ask that you try and buy, beg, or borrow a copy of *Love Re-membered*. The background information and descriptions are important: the words are but one part of a whole celebration which also includes space and movement, furnishings and costume, roles and relationships, art and music. Thinking through these things helps us to plan acts of worship that have their own particular style and coherence.

Appendix 5

Some miscellaneous Collects

1

Ever-present God,
    faithful in each moment,
    for whom day and night are alike,
do not let our hearts be troubled,
    but fill us with such confidence and joy
        that we may sleep in peace
        and wake to your presence.
We pray this after the pattern of Jesus
    and in the power of the Spirit.

2

Liberating Presence,
    loosening the chains that hold us fast,
    weaning us from the addictions
        to which we fall prey,
keep us compassionate and firm,
    with ourselves and with others,
that together we may inherit
    your domain of true freedom.
We pray this after the pattern of Jesus
    and in the power of the Spirit.

3

Living Presence, quiet and hidden,
   whose silences speaks clearer than any words,
keep us from the trap of thinking
   that the louder we shout
      the more genuine is our faith
   and the more fulsome is our praise,
so that we may, with tact and tenderness,
   greet others from your silence
      deep within our hearts
We pray this after the pattern of Jesus
   and in the power of the Spirit.

4

Living Presence of the spiralling dance,
   exuberant in delight, generous in gift,
loosen our stiff bodies,
   so stingy and grudging,
that we may dance again
   with sparkle in our eyes and joy in our hearts.
We pray this after the pattern of Jesus
   and in the power of the Spirit.

5

Creating Presence,
   yet friend to each and every one of us,
giving us our homes and households,
   our communities and our cities,
disturb us when we feel most settled,
   and steady us when we wander restlessly,
that in moments of stillness and reflection
   we may come together in gratitude for one another
   and in fulfilment of a destiny beyond our imagining.
We pray this after the pattern of Jesus
   and in the power of the Spirit.

6

Living Communion, Three-in-One, One-in-Three,
   drawing us into your inner life of love,
   where hurts are healed and loneliness transformed,
may the fitful tremblings of our prayer
   move through the world with compassion,
that someone in prison, neglected and forgotten,
   may know at least a moment's respite from despair,
   and be touched by the gift of kindness
     when least expected.
We pray this after the pattern of Jesus
   and in the power of the Spirit.

7

Mysterious Presence,
   of whom we are unaware
     when afraid of the power
       of the storm that destroys,
     and when terrified of the power
       of the love that transfigures,
speak to us in accents of encouragement,
   that we be not afraid,
   that we be of good courage,
   that we may know that you are with us.
We pray this after the pattern of Jesus
   and in the power of the Spirit.

8

Living Presence, constant and faithful,
   surprising us with how reliable you are,
alert us to your presence
   in the trustworthiness of so many people
     in their repeated tasks for the common good,
deepen in us a sense of wonder at this mystery,

APPENDIX 5

   the marvel of the everyday,
and give us thankful hearts
   for the passionate and limitless giving of yourself
      to us and all the world,
after the pattern of Jesus
   and in the power of the Spirit.

9

Living Presence,
   bewildering and mysterious in your ways,
   into whose silence we hurl all that is unresolved,
in the midst of our questions
   deepen our trust
and in the midst of our trust
   keep our questions alive,
that our eyes may be opened to your trustworthiness
   and our hearts purified to will one thing,
that we may indeed follow your way
   through and beyond all that perplexes us
   from which we cannot escape.
We pray this after the pattern of Jesus
   and in the power of the Spirit.

10

Living Presence,
   close to us in the Spirit of Jesus,
   decisive clue to your love that has no end,
renew in us the steady hope
   that even the power of death
      cannot sever us from your presence.
We pray this after the pattern of Jesus
   and in the power of the Spirit.

11

Living Presence in the midst of the ruins
   of the temples we build,
Living Presence of the empty silent places,
   whose walls have fallen
     because our vision is too narrow,
open our ears to hear them speaking to us
   with strange eloquence,
   of what is always beyond us
   and cannot be shaped by what we humans build,
so that we resist the temptation
   to cage you, to control you,
   and to construct an image that replaces you.
We pray this after the pattern of Jesus
   and in the power of the Spirit.

12

Living Presence,
   whose lasting city is a community of the peace
   that flows not from victory but from justice,
sharpen our judgement
   that we may discern how to build wisely,
     protecting and shaping city and home,
       farm and wilderness,
       partnerships and friendships,
   all in harmony with your will,
so that they alone become
   the temples of your presence,
   the places of our prayer,
   and the new Jerusalem
     for which we yearn and long.
We pray this after the pattern of Jesus
   and in the power of the Spirit.

13

Hidden Presence,
   whom we do not notice as we pass by,
   ignoring you in the forlorn and despairing,
give us the vision to see you in those we reject,
   who hold us steadily with the eyes
     of those who know the worst,
   yet whose arms stretch forward
     to embrace us with your mercy,
   if we will but receive their gift.
We pray this after the pattern of Jesus
   and in the power of the Spirit.

14

Mysterious yet incarnate Presence,
   whose glory shines through the heavens,
   and whose handiwork the universe declares,
empower each and everyone
   to strive for emancipation
     from the kingdom of mammon
     and the empire of worldly power,
   and with our energy and skill
     craft what is beautiful and useful
       in your commonwealth of gift and grace.
We pray this after the pattern of Jesus
   and in the power of the Spirit.

15

Living Presence to the desert pilgrims,
    to those who are wearied
        by montonous days of sun or cloud,
    who are battered
        by the monstrous whirling winds,
surprise us yet with a monstrance of wonder,
    a revelation of love,
    an oasis of refreshment,
    a taste of the harvest,
    a moment of grace.
We pray this after the pattern of Jesus
    and in the power of the Spirit.

16

Compassionate Presence,
    aflame with yearning,
    alive in Jesus to heal by word and touch,
empower us in the Spirit to bring
    words of kindness to the broken-hearted
    and a cooling touch to the fevered,
that together we may be made whole,
    raised to life in the power of your love.
We pray this in the Spirit of the universal Christ, incarnate and
    glorified,
humanity alive in you for ever.